LEVEL 3

The Award in Education and Training

A PRACTICAL GUIDE

Michelle Dawes
Jane Owen

eboru

The publisher gratefully acknowledges the permission of copyright holders to reproduce copyright material.

Cover image and title page: © plutmaverick/Shutterstock

p6 iStock.com/SolStock p.23 StockSmartStart/Shutterstock; p24 iStock.com/Edwin Tan; p30/31 iStock.com/mayrum; p40 (top) iStock.com/northlightimages; p40 (middle) iStock.com/Daisy-Daisy; p40 (bottom) 123RF.com; p41 (top) Andrey_Popov/Shutterstock; p41(bottom) KatMoys/Shutterstock; p51 iStock.com/sturti; p55 iStock.com/izusek; p58 iStock.com/Cecilie_Arcurs; p64 Monkey Business Images//Shutterstock; p76 iStock.com/andresr; p102 iStock.com/ JohnnyGreig; p113 iStock.com/MR1805

Every effort has been made to trace copyright holders and to obtain their permission for the use of copyright material. The publisher will be glad to make arrangements with any copyright holder it has not been possible to contact.

Copyright © 2024 Michelle Dawes and Jane Owen

The Author's right to be identified as author of this work has been asserted in accordance with the Copyright, Designs and Patents Act 1988

All rights reserved. No part of this publication may be reproduced, distributed, or transmitted in any form or by any means, including photocopying, recording, or other electronic or mechanical methods, without the prior written permission of the publisher, or under licence from the Copyright Licensing Agency. See www.cla.co.uk for more details.

First edition 2024. Impression 10 9 8 7 6 5 4 3 2

ISBN 978-1-917048-02-6

Whilst every effort has been made to ensure all information in this book is correct, the publisher shall not be liable for any loss of profit or any other commercial damages, including but not limited to special, incidental, consequential, personal, or other damages, due to any information or advice contained in this book.

If you do spot any errors in this book you can alert the publisher at: enquiries@eboru.com

Ordering Information

Special discounts are available for class set purchases by schools, colleges and others. For details, contact the publisher at: orders@eboru.com

Trade orders: copies of this book are available through the normal wholesalers. For any queries please contact: orders@eboru.com

www.eboru.com

Acknowledgements

Michelle and Jane would like to thank their partners, Paul and Steve, and their family for their unwavering support during the writing of this book. They would like to acknowledge the encouragement and support from James Staniforth, Principal and CEO of Shrewsbury College. They would also like to acknowledge the guidance provided by Elizabeth Wilkinson, MBE, who supported on the topic of neurodiversity.

Introduction

The purpose of this book is to provide a practical guide to successfully completing the Level 3 Award in Education & Training. Michelle and Jane are seasoned teachers on the level 3 programme and have successfully delivered it for many years to generations of teachers and trainers, helping them to develop their knowledge and experience and apply theory to practice.

The writing builds on these years of teaching adults in the post-compulsory sector, helping them shape a career in teaching or training.

There are sections that feature well established and well-known theories, along with newer ideas and terminology.

The chapters of the book will provide you with the foundations to design, deliver and assess effective teaching/training sessions. More importantly, you will start to understand what makes an effective session for different learners, which in turn will lead to a deeper understanding of the craft of teaching and training.

Features in this book

Activity
What else do you think would be expected of a teacher/trainer by your organisation?

Activities throughout help to consolidate understanding

Key tip
Early familiarisation with the policy and

Helpful hints for learning and practice

cyberbullying any bullying or abusive behaviour that takes place online

Key terms

Case Study
Let's explore this further. Misbehaviour or disruption in the classroom can detract from learning. Knowing what processes

Case Studies will help you to apply knowledge to practical situations

Reflection Question
What are your views and experiences of mobile phones in the classroom?

Designed to develop your reflective practice skills

See section 1.2 in this unit for more details about legislation

Make links across the book and qualification

In the classroom
Continuing with the swearing theme, the following situation is a real example of establishing boundaries. A group of

Examples of how concepts in the book may be observed or experienced in a real classroom

Ideas for teaching...
Here are some more ideas of how we can promote equality in the classroom, based on the

Practical ways in which you could incorporate ideas into real lessons

Contents

Introduction

Chapter 1 Understanding roles, responsibilities and relationships in education and training

LO1 Understand the teaching role and responsibilities in education and training — 7
1.1 Explain the teaching role and responsibilities in education and training — 7
1.2 Summarise key aspects of legislation, regulatory requirements and codes of practice relating to own role and responsibilities — 15
1.3 Explain ways to promote equality and value diversity — 23
1.4 Explain why it is important to identify and meet individual learner needs — 30

LO2 Understand ways to maintain a safe and supportive learning environment — 39
2.1 Explain ways to maintain a safe and supportive learning environment — 39
2.2 Explain why it is important to promote appropriate behaviour and respect for others — 49

LO3 Understand the relationships between teachers and other professionals in education and training — 52
3.1 Explain how the teaching role involves working with other professionals — 52
3.2 Explain the boundaries between the teaching role and other professional roles — 55
3.3 Describe points of referral to meet the individual needs of learners — 56

Chapter 2 Understand and using inclusive teaching and learning approaches in education and training

LO1 Understanding inclusive teaching and learning approaches in education and training — 59
1.1 Describe features of inclusive teaching and learning approaches in education and training — 59
1.2 Compare the strengths and limitations of teaching and learning approaches used in own area of specialism in relation to meeting individual learner needs — 64
1.3 Explain why it is important to provide opportunities for learners to develop their English, mathematics, ICT and wider skills — 66

LO2 Understand ways to create an inclusive teaching and learning environment — 68
2.1 Explain why it is important to create an inclusive teaching and learning environment. — 68
2.2 Explain why it is important to select teaching and learning approaches, resources and assessment methods to meet individual learner needs — 70
2.3 Explain ways to engage and motivate learners — 71
2.4 Summarise ways to establish ground rules with learners — 74

LO3 Be able to plan inclusive teaching and learning — 76
3.1 Devise an inclusive teaching and learning plan — 77
3.2 Justify own selection of teaching and learning approaches, resources and assessment methods in relation to meeting individual learner needs — 88

LO4 Be able to deliver inclusive teaching and learning — 90
4.1 Use teaching and learning approaches, resources and assessment methods to meet individual learner needs — 90
4.2 Communicate with learners in ways that meet their individual needs — 92
4.3 Provide constructive feedback to learners to meet their individual needs — 95

LO5 Be able to evaluate the delivery of inclusive teaching and learning — 98
5.1 Review the effectiveness of own delivery of inclusive teaching and learning — 98
5.2 Identify areas for improvement in own delivery of inclusive teaching and learning — 98

Chapter 3 Understanding Assessment in Education and Training

LO1 Understand types and methods of assessment used in education and training — 103
1.1 Explain the purposes of types of assessment used in education and training — 103
1.2 Describe characteristics of different methods of assessment in education and training — 107
1.3 Compare the strengths and limitations of different assessment methods in relation to meeting individual learner needs — 107
1.4 Explain how different assessment methods can be adapted to meet individual needs — 110

LO2 Understand how to involve learners and others in the assessment process — 112
2.1 Explain why it is important to involve learners and others in the assessment process — 112
2.2 Explain the role and use of peer- and self-assessment in the assessment process — 115
2.3 Identify sources of information that should be made available to learners and others involved in the assessment process — 115

LO3 Understand the role and use of constructive feedback in the assessment process — 117
3.1 Describe key features of constructive feedback — 117
3.2 Explain how constructive feedback contributes to the assessment process — 118
3.3 Explain ways to give constructive feedback to learners — 119

LO4 Understand requirements for keeping records of assessment in education and training — 122
4.1 Explain the need to keep records of assessment of learning — 122
4.2 Summarise the requirements for keeping records of assessment in an organisation — 122

References — 125

Appendix 1 — 127
Artificial Intelligence (AI) — 127
Sustainability — 129

Appendix 2 — 130

Index — 131

Chapter 1 Understanding roles, responsibilities and relationships in education and training

By the end of this chapter, you will be able to describe the roles and responsibilities of the teacher and trainer. You will also know how to create a safe learning environment within the relevant legal and ethical frameworks, understand the roles of other professionals in education and training, and know about the boundaries between your own role and those professionals.

LO1: Understand the teaching role and responsibilities in education and training.

LO2: Understand ways to maintain a safe and supportive learning environment.

LO3: Understand the relationships between teachers and other professionals in education and training.

LO1 Understand the teaching role and responsibilities in education and training

1.1 Explain the teaching role and responsibilities in education and training.

1.2 Summarise key aspects of legislation, regulatory requirements and codes of practice relating to own role and responsibilities.

1.3 Explain ways to promote equality and value diversity.

1.4 Explain why it is important to identify and meet individual learner needs.

1.1 Explain the teaching role and responsibilities in education and training

A good starting point is to understand the difference between roles and responsibilities. They are closely linked but:

- your role is the task you perform
- responsibilities are what you are accountable for

We can think about roles and responsibilities in relation to the following:

- The learner.
- The educational organisation.
- Legislation, policies and procedures.
- Professional boundaries.

The learner

Throughout this book, you will be encouraged to be learner-centred, to focus on the needs of the individuals you will be teaching or training, and to be as flexible as possible to suit the learner. So, the learner is the first stakeholder to consider. Also note that when we use the term 'learner' we are referring to a person who is receiving the teaching or training, so they could also be termed as a student, delegate, participant or individual.

By completing all the suggested activities in this section you will have comprehensive notes to complete your assessment on the roles and responsibilities of a teacher.

Activity

'What will the learner need from me?'

Think about this question. Give yourself a few minutes to list what you think the learner will expect from you. You can make these points specific to your current role if you have one. If you are not yet in a role, consider what it is you would expect from your teacher or trainer.

LO1

Your answers to the activity may include some of the following:

- To be knowledgeable in my subject.
- To arrive, start and end sessions on time.
- To be clear about the content and the requirements.
- To ensure the environment is conducive to the course or training.

You may have thought of some other points too. Your list may be lengthy or short. This doesn't matter as long as you have a list that you understand and can reasonably explain.

Activity

To take things a step further, expand the list to consider not only 'what' but 'why'.

Look at the list you made in the previous activity. For each point, write a sentence or two explaining why the learner will need this from you.

What does the learner expect from me?	Why?

The educational organisation

Now you need to think about what is expected of a teacher/trainer by the organisation they work for.

Activity

List what you think your organisation will expect you to do in a typical lesson.

Your list may contain some of the following:

- Keeping a register of attendance.
- Marking students' written assignments/presentations etc. in a timely manner.
- Finding and supplying specific teaching resources that are required.
- Prepare tasks.
- Prepare resources.
- Share information.
- Teach key knowledge.

Your list probably relates to specific teaching tasks that take place in the classroom.

Activity

Look at the list you made in the last activity. For each point, write a sentence or two explaining why you think this would be expected of a teacher/trainer.

What does the organisation expect from me?	Why?

Teachers and trainers also have responsibilities that go beyond teaching in a classroom. Now you need to think about some of the broader aspects of delivering a course. Some of the points will be specific to the organisation you are working with.

Activity

What else do you think would be expected of a teacher/trainer by your organisation?

Your list for this activity may include things such as:
- Ensuring the environment is safe and conducive to learning.
- Completing evaluations of the programme or course.
- Making sure the right technology is available.
- Selecting guest speakers where appropriate and ensuring they are available.
- Attending meetings.

These examples are not an exhaustive list, but provide an idea of some other features of a teaching/training role.

Activity

Look at the list you made. For each point, write a sentence or two explaining why you think this would be expected of a teacher/trainer.

What else does the organisation expect from me?	Why?

Now there are three separate lists, we can think about combining them together.

> **Activity**
>
> Consider the three lists you have made. Merge any ideas from the three lists that are linked. Now, create a new table with the following headings, and place each of your ideas into one of the two columns:
>
> | Roles | Responsibilities |
> |---|---|
> | | |
> | | |
> | | |
> | | |
> | | |
> | | |

Legislation, policies and procedures

The roles and responsibilities of a teacher are also informed by:

- organisational policies
- organisational procedures
- legislation (i.e. laws)

Policies are rules and guidelines of an organisation that explain the principles and stance the organisation is taking on a particular aspect. For example, every educational organisation will have a policy on equality and diversity. They will have many other policies too.

Procedures are the finer detail that explain how the policies will be followed and implemented.

It is advisable to take time to find out about the policies and procedures that are in place in your organisation. It is wise to ask your line manager or Human Resource department about the key policies that cover things such as:

- Safeguarding
- Prevent
- Code of conduct for learners
- Complaints policy
- Anti-bullying/Harassment policy

This is not an exhaustive list – there may be many different policies and procedures in place which will be specific to each type of organisation or educational setting you are placed in.

Familiarity with organisational policies and procedures can help guide your classroom management and the pastoral support you provide for your learners. It is far better to be proactive and learn about these policies and procedures as soon as possible, as they can help to inform your teaching and learning strategies and build a foundation as you develop your skills and knowledge.

> **Key tip**
> Early familiarisation with the policy and procedures of your organisation will be time well-spent and will provide a framework for your responses in challenging situations.

> **Case Study**
>
> Misbehaviour or disruption in the classroom can detract from learning. Knowing what policies and procedures are in place can support you in the methods you use to deal with behaviour. In a college setting, some types of behaviour will result in instant suspension from the course.
>
> Consider how you would deal with the following scenario:
>
> You are in an engineering workshop and have a student who has decided to wave a power tool in the face of another student in a foolish way. The student is acting carelessly and you witness this behaviour.
>
> - How would you react?
> - What would you say to the student?
> - What would be the consequences for this action?
>
> For many colleges, this would be seen as gross misconduct as the student brandishing the power tool has broken significant health and safety rules. Exactly how a college would deal with this incident would depend on their policies and procedures. You would need to know about the code of conduct and behavioural policies and procedures.
>
> In this instance the student was immediately suspended, parents were called to advise of the suspension and why, and the student was given a week to 'cool off' before meeting with a conduct panel. The panel reviewed the behaviour and listened to the teacher's and student's version of events, before making a final decision. The outcome was that the student was given a final written warning and if any further disruptive behaviour was carried out, the student would be withdrawn from the course.
>
> Many situations in the classroom will involve several policies and procedures.

Activity

Write a list of some things that an organisation might cover with its policies and procedures. Compare your list with other members of the class and discuss.

Legislation is a very important aspect of a teacher's roles and responsibilities. There are certain laws which all teachers/trainers must be familiar with. These laws mean that teachers/trainers have legal responsibilities in their role. We will explore some key legislation for teachers/trainers in more detail in the next section of the book, LO 1.2.

Establishing professional boundaries

To fulfil the role and responsibilities of the teacher/trainer, we need to be clear about the professional boundaries that we establish with learners to ensure they are compliant with legislation and organisational policies. Professional boundaries will often set the tone of the relationship between the teacher and the learner, and can shape the learning experience for individuals.

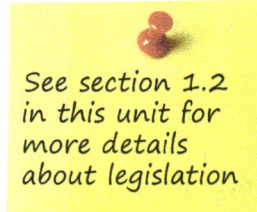

See section 1.2 in this unit for more details about legislation

LO1

Before undertaking and delivering any course, you should first consider your professional boundaries.

Consider the following questions:

- What do you want the culture of your classroom to be?
- How do you want to establish the relationship between you and your learners?
- What behaviour is/isn't acceptable?

It can save time if you are clear from the start about:

- behaviour you will accept
- how you will address behaviour that is not acceptable, and communicate these expectations to the learners so that they are clear and understand what is expected.

Activity

Let's take a simple example: swearing in the classroom.

- What is your stance on this?
- Which words are acceptable, if any, and which words aren't?
- Is swearing acceptable in the context of your subject area?

Some professions and workplace cultures may accept swearing but others may not. Later in the book we will explore the methods you can use to establish workable boundaries within the teaching and training environment. However, be clear about your own professional and personal boundaries in the first instance, to help shape and develop the culture of your classroom and the learners' experience.

In the classroom

Continuing with the swearing theme, the following situation is a real example of establishing boundaries. A group of engineering students were inherited by a different teacher. All were employed and had day release to complete their Higher National qualification. The culture of the group was to swear freely and without regard for others. The teacher was not keen on this behaviour. They explained why it was not appropriate, how it may not be acceptable in some workplaces and asked what would stop them. They said a swear box would help. Over the coming weeks, the group collected about £20 but, more importantly, the students had become aware of their swearing, reduced it dramatically and agreed that the learning environment had become more respectful and purposeful. By having a clear personal and professional boundary, this situation was dealt with swiftly and provided a foundation for expectations within the learning environment. (The £20 went to charity.)

> **Case Study**
>
> **When you know the attendees...**
>
> It is the first session with a new group of 12 learners. The subject is one that you are very familiar with, so you are confident with the content. Two of the learners are personal friends and have already approached you to ask if they could leave a couple of hours early as they have a social event. They have texted you on your personal mobile number and they have intimated that you will be lenient on them and be able to provide many of the answers to any coursework they need to complete.
>
> - Identify the potential problems in this scenario.
> - What are the key issues in relation to your role and responsibilities?
> - What specific strategies would you suggest to help solve the issues identified?
> - What would your employer expect from you in this situation?
> - What would other learners expect from you?

Exploring your own boundaries, and knowing how you want the culture in your classroom or training room to be, can really help you to set ground rules and foster a positive learning environment. Consider how the environment can be nurtured to foster an atmosphere conducive to learning and ensure you are clear in your communication with your learners or delegates about what is or isn't acceptable.

> **Case Study**
>
> **Mobile Phones**
>
> It is the first session together with a new group of learners/delegates. One learner asks your view on the use of mobile phones in the classroom.
>
> - What is your response?
> - What could be the consequences to your response?
> - What are the benefits to the use of mobile phones in the classroom?
> - What are the pitfalls?

Whatever your view on the use of mobile phones in the classroom, it will be controversial to someone. At a time when the government are exploring the option of banning mobile phones in schools and linking the use of phones to behaviour, it is sensible to explore their use for adult learners. Ask staff and students questions around how learning can be enhanced by using technology and considering what levels of distractions they can cause.

> **Key tip**
>
> You do not need to answer all questions about classroom management on your own. You can discuss with your learners how they want issues to be managed. Remember, though, you do need to have your own boundaries identified in advance so that you can help influence the outcome and achieve a balanced and workable solution for all, and one that fits into your learning environment.

LO1

To conclude this section check you have completed the following and then start your action plan to develop your skills further:

- Have you listed features of your role?
- Have you identified your responsibilities?
- Are you able to explain why they are important aspects?
- What organisational policies and procedures are important for you to know about?
- Have you established your preferred boundaries?
- How will you introduce these to your learners/delegates?

Reflection Question

What is your view and experiences of mobile phones in the classroom?

role the tasks that are performed

responsibility the things that you are accountable for

policy the rules, guidelines, and principles of an organisation

procedure the processes used to ensure the policy is adhered to

boundaries guidelines to work towards that support the process in a professional manner

1.2 Summarise key aspects of legislation, regulatory requirements and codes of practice relating to own role and responsibilities

Introduction to legislation, regulatory requirements, and codes of practice

Legislation, regulations and codes of practice underpin your roles and responsibilities as a teacher/trainer. Let's define each of these in turn:

- **Legislation** – laws that are passed by Parliament.
- **Regulatory requirements** – rules containing the details of how laws will be implemented in practice by a governing body.
- **Codes of practice** – a practical guide on how to follow and comply with legal duties.

Legislation and regulations

It is crucial that you have knowledge of the key legislation and regulations that govern practice and impact on teaching and training. Ignorance is no defence.

Laws and regulations change frequently so it is important to ensure you have strategies for keeping up to date with any changes. Organisations will often provide training as they also have a legal obligation to ensure they and their staff comply with changes.

Legislation can be considered a 'dry' subject. Quite often when it is introduced, eyes immediately begin to glaze over! However, in order to become a safe and effective teacher you will need to be aware of the legislation that supports and governs your roles. This point cannot be stressed enough.

We will start with an overview of some of the key sections of legislation that you need to know about. However, remember that there may be other relevant laws that are specific to your workplace and your region.

The main legislation we need to consider is as follows:

1. Health & Safety at Work Act (1974)
    * Reporting of Injuries, Diseases and Dangerous Occurrences Regulations (2013) RIDDOR
    * Control of Substances Hazardous to Health (COSHH) Regulations
2. Data Protection Act (2018)
    * General Data Protection Regulations (2018) GDPR
3. The Children Act (1989, 2004), Children and Social Work Act (2017)
4. Safeguarding & Vulnerable Groups Act (2006)
    * Keeping children safe in education (2022)
5. The Equality Act (2010)
6. The Education Act (2011)
7. Counter-Terrorism & Security Act (2015) – incudes 'Prevent' strategy
8. Copyright Designs & Patent Act (1988)
9. Freedom of Information Act (2000)
10. Bribery Act (2010)

Health & Safety at Work Act (1974)

The H&SAW Act covers health and safety in the workplace. It covers both employer and employee responsibilities. The Act ensures that employers provide a safe place to work and that individuals are trained how to act safely. It also ensures that employers have developed a health and safety policy and obliges them to carry out risk assessments.

Some of the main responsibilities of an employee are:

- To take reasonable care of yourself and others.
- To cooperate with the employer on matters of health and safety. This means undertaking any necessary training, following any given guidelines, wearing any necessary protective equipment etc.
- To not interfere with health and safety equipment or signs.

Relevance to teachers and trainers: Accidents can occur in all workplaces. Common accidents or injuries in classrooms relate to incorrectly lifting heavy objects, poor posture at desks, and tripping over obstacles in poorly laid-out rooms.

RIDDOR (2013)

The Reporting of Injuries, Diseases and Dangerous Occurrences Regulations (2013) makes it a legal requirement for an employer to record and report any accidents or incidents that take place in the workplace.

Relevance to teachers and trainers: As an employee, it is your responsibility to tell your line manager about any accidents or incidents you are involved in or witness.

Control of Substances Hazardous to Health (COSHH) (2002)

These regulations cover employer and employee responsibilities when there is any potential for exposure to harmful substances. They aim to ensure that such substances are handled and disposed of in such a way that they do not harm individuals or the environment. There is not a definitive list of substances because it depends what is done with them. For instance, someone washing dishes all day without gloves would constantly expose their hands to water, which would cause long-term skin problems. Using water in this way would fall under the COSHH regulations.

Relevance to teachers and trainers: Some departments in a college or training organisation are more likely to use substances that fall under the COSHH regulations. For instance, if you are teaching or training in an engineering, motor vehicle, beauty, or catering environment, to name but a few, it will be important to be aware of the guidelines around COSHH. Employers and employees who breach the regulations can be subjected to an unlimited fine.

Data Protection Act (2018) & GDPR

The Data Protection Act (2018) implements the General Data Protection Regulation (GDPR) which sets out strict rules around data protection.

- Organisations must gain consent from individuals before processing their personal information.
- They must make sure that the information is used fairly, transparently, and lawfully.
- The data should only be used for specific stated purposes and should not be kept for longer than necessary.
- There is stronger legal protection for sensitive information such as ethnicity, race, health, religious beliefs, political opinions, trade union membership and sexual orientation.

There are six principles that lie at the centre of the regulations which aim to protect individuals and their personal information. The Information Commissioners Office has a useful website that breaks down some of the legislation and offers more detail around the expectations. It also explains why this Act is important and how it can be followed.

Relevance to teachers and trainers: Within our roles as trainers or teachers, the GDPR governs the way we hold data and information about individuals, how it is shared and how it is used. This information can be online (for instance, in emails or spreadsheets) or offline (e.g. hard copies files in filing cabinets). There are potentially heavy fines for organisations that do not implement the principles in full, so all staff must follow them.

The Children Act (1989, 2004)
Children and Social Work Act (2017)

The Children Act (1989) is the basis of the current child protection system. It required local authorities to safeguard children in their area, and promote their welfare, by providing a range of services. The 2004 Act was introduced to improve and integrate children's services run by different departments or bodies. It requires these different departments to talk to one another to ensure a child's safety and welfare are the top priority when multi-disciplinary teams are working with a child or family. It also defines the roles and responsibilities of safeguarding partners (such as the local authority, NHS and the police). All relevant parties need to share information and use resources to make the best decision to support the child and/or family. The Act established a Children's Commissioner in England and created Local Safeguarding Children's Boards.

The Children and Social Work Act (2017) made some amendments to further improve safeguarding across multi-disciplinary teams. It also focused on children and young people who were being looked after by the local authority, or had previously been looked after.

Relevance to teachers and trainers: Anyone working with children need to understand their safeguarding and welfare responsibilities. Mandatory training is provided by organisations to ensure compliance of both the setting and the staff.

Safeguarding & Vulnerable Groups Act (2006)

This Act was passed with the aim of preventing unsuitable people working with children and vulnerable adults. It created one single list of people barred from working with children, and one list for vulnerable adults. The Independent Safeguarding Authority (ISA) was established to decide who should be placed on each list. In 2012 the ISA's role was merged into a new body called the Disclosure and Barring Service (DBS), which maintains responsibilities for the lists. All staff working with children and vulnerable adults are required to have a DBS check to deem whether they are on either list, and therefore whether they are suitable to work with these groups.

Relevance to teachers and trainers: All staff working with children (under the age of 18) or vulnerable adults must be DBS checked. Training will support staff to understand their role in keeping children and vulnerable adults safe.

Keeping children safe in education (KCSIE)

This statutory guidance is updated annually and is essential reading for all staff working within a school or college setting. This ensures that everyone knows their safeguarding responsibilities.

Relevance to teachers and trainers: This is relevant to anyone working with anyone under 18.

The Equality Act (2010)

This Act legally protects people from discrimination in the workplace and in wider society. There are nine characteristics that are protected by the Act:

- Age
- Disability
- Gender reassignment
- Marriage or civil partnership
- Pregnancy and maternity
- Race
- Religion or belief
- Sex
- Sexual Orientation

The Citizen's Advice Bureau define discrimination as 'treating you unfairly because of who you are'. The Act makes it illegal to be discriminated against, for any of the nine characteristics, by a range of organisations including employers and businesses, schools and colleges, and other public sector organisations and health care providers.

Relevance to teachers and trainers: Any organisation you are involved with has a legal responsibility not to discriminate. They will have equality and diversity statements and policies for employees to follow, to ensure it does not happen.

The Education Act (2011)

The Education Act (2011) aimed to help raise standards in education. It includes powers to help teachers address poor behaviour and tackle underperformance, and also increased schools' accountability. Rules about managing colleges were also changed, and post-16 funding was focused towards under-19s, apprenticeships, and numeracy and literacy qualifications. It also scrapped a number of education bodies performing various roles, and transferred their powers to Department for Education.

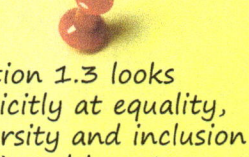

Section 1.3 looks explicitly at equality, diversity and inclusion (EDI) and how to embed it in teaching and training.

Relevance to teachers and trainers: Provides an understanding of why certain post-16 qualifications are funded.

Counter-Terrorism Act and Security Act (2015)

The Counter-Terrorism and Security Act was passed in 2015 to help respond to the threat of terrorism within the UK. The links to education are through the 'Prevent' strategy. This is one of the strategies the UK government introduced which aims to prevent the radicalisation of children and vulnerable young people, and stop them being drawn into terrorism.

The Department for Education (DfE) provided guidance for schools and childcare providers to help them:

- understand the implications of the Prevent duty,
- demonstrate compliance with the duty
- protect children and vulnerable young people from the risk of radicalisation and extremism. This also requires the building of resilience to radicalisation and promoting fundamental British values.

Educational settings will deliver mandatory training to raise awareness and help inform teachers about their obligations. In addition to this, the Society for Education & Training www.set.et-foundation.co.uk also offer CPD around safeguarding and Prevent, and regularly offer sessions to support schools and colleges.

Relevance to teachers and trainers: All education providers need to be aware of the Prevent duty.

Copyright Designs & Patent Act (1988)

This law protects creative works and stops others from using them without the creator's permission. This is called copyright. Creative works can be text, music, images or other artistic works. Copyright protection is given automatically, and a creator can mark their work with © along with their name and the year of creation. This aims to protect those resources.

Relevance to teachers and trainers: This law means that text, music and images from any source, including the internet, can't just be copied and used without asking for permission. However, most educational organisations hold a photocopying license which permits a teacher to copy up to 5% of a book or one chapter, whichever is greater. You should check if your institution has signed up to the licence, which is run by the Copyright Licencing Agency (CLA) www.cla.co.uk

Freedom of Information Act (2000)

This Act makes provision for the disclosure of information that is held by public authorities. It gives individuals and organisations the right to request access to information that is held by the public organisation. It covers official documents, drafts, emails, notes, CCTV recordings, and anything else that is recorded and held.

Relevance to teachers and trainers: This law applies to schools, colleges and universities. As an educational or training professional, be mindful of the records you keep and the notes that you take. Would you be comfortable with a member of the public reading them?

The Bribery Act (2010)

Perhaps an odd one to identify as something of concern within an educational setting but the purpose of the Bribery Act is to prove that organisations are free from bribery and corruption. As a result, all UK organisations will have a policy around bribery and corruption.

Whilst it may sound like an unusual Act to highlight, consider the following real-life example:

> **In the classroom**
>
> Several years ago, I was gifted a rather nice bottle of champagne from an appreciative student who had just completed his course. The organisation I worked for had just introduced a process to address the requirements of the Bribery Act and the upper threshold for any gifts was £25. Anything over this amount had to be declared. I duly notified the administrator that I had been given a gift as a 'thank you' and that I thought it was over the value threshold. I expected it to be noted down and told to enjoy my gift. But no! It was taken off me and raffled off at the Christmas party. As you can imagine I was disappointed, but learned that the policies were in place to prevent students influencing a teacher's marks or views of that student. Sadly, the fact that the course had finished and I had no further influence was not taken into consideration. (As you can see, I am over it, almost).

Safeguarding

Depending on your setting and your role, some legislation will be more important than others. If you are in education, then Acts 3-7 (page 15) will be extremely relevant. Usually, your organisation will offer further training to ensure that individuals understand their legal obligations around safeguarding legislation.

Safeguarding is key in an education setting and drives a lot of policies and procedures. The degree to which you are involved will vary depending on your role and your organisation but make sure you are aware of the basic principles of safeguarding.

A described above, the government publishes key guidelines on the topic. For instance, 'Keeping children safe in education' is updated regularly and is freely available through the government website. The document sets out your legal requirements as well as recommended tasks. Changes from the previous year are highlighted.

Activity

1. Check your organisation's requirements in relation to safeguarding children and vulnerable groups.

2. List the legislation that you think will apply to you in your role.

Consider the impact this has on:

- You
- Your learners
- Your organisation

In the classroom

Whilst we have listed the most common relevant legislation, there may be other legislation that you need to consider in your particular role or location. For instance, I am based on the border between England and Wales and therefore I need to consider implications of the Welsh Language Act (1993). Other regions or roles may be impacted by different legislation.

Policies, Procedures and Codes of Practice

All organisations have a set of policies and procedures that will impact on your teaching or training. Some will be introduced at your induction. Others you will come across whilst working in your role.

Quite often, familiarity with a particular policy or procedure is driven by necessity. For example, if you are struggling with poor behaviour within the classroom, you will need to be familiar with the behavioural code of practice that has been set out by your organisation, so that you can follow the process.

Take time to familiarise yourself with the policies and procedures that are available. Here is a list of possible examples:

- Equality & Diversity statement
- Disability statement
- Visitor policy
- E-Safety policy & procedure
- Social media policy
- Criminal convictions policy
- Freedom of information policy
- Complaints policy
- Data protection policy
- Behaviour/Conduct policy

You can probably see how these examples tend to support the legislation that is in place. They also set out expectations, standards and processes to ensure fairness and consistency when dealing with a situation or request.

1.3 Explain ways to promote equality and value diversity

What do we mean by equality and diversity in education and training?

Equality is sometimes described as creating an 'even playing field'. However, the creation of an equal space for learners to thrive and produce their best work can look very different for each person. The key is understanding the individual and their set of circumstances. Equality in the classroom can often be described as equity, where we consider how to give fair access to opportunities, rather than everyone being treated the same.

EQUALITY **EQUITY**

Diversity is the celebration of differences. It is created by getting to know learners so that we understand their differences in culture, background, aspirations and learning needs.

Why is equality and diversity important in education?

There was a time, not so long ago, when:

- learners were expected to fit into the classroom, regardless of their learning difficulties, their background and culture, or their personal aspirations
- learners who did not fit the mould were ostracised
- learners were punished for not trying hard enough if they could not keep up with the work
- learners were labelled in one way or another.

Perhaps you remember these times. Or perhaps you were unfortunate enough to have experienced this yourself.

When we think about these situations and the individual experiences, we can see how they would have a deep impact on these learners' views of education.

Legislation encourages and enforces changes to the systems and processes within education. We can clearly see the effect of such changes in the language around disabilities: many words used freely 30 years ago to describe someone with a learning or physical disability are no longer acceptable. It is now rightly recognised that they cause distress, disengagement with education, and are discriminative in practice.

However, legislation alone is not enough. Therefore it is important that, as education providers, we set standards of acceptable behaviour and expectations for all interactions. Organisational codes of practice are based on the principals of:

- respect for differences
- understanding individual needs.

As teachers, the ultimate goal is to create an inclusive learning environment where everyone feels safe, confident to be who they are, are valued and understood, and can fulfil their potential. Inclusivity within education and training gives all learners the best opportunity to be successful and to progress to further learning and development.

Promoting equality and diversity

Stakeholders in education

The Equality Act (2010) doesn't in itself create fairness and equity. The pursuit of equality within education and training combines the work of many different parties:

- The Department for Education
- Awarding bodies
- Ofsted
- The Education and Training Foundation (ETF)
- Education and training providers
- Leadership teams
- Individual teachers/trainers.

> The Equality Act (2010) covers many aspects of equality in the classroom, particularly around the protected characteristics (See LO 1.2).

The ETF's Professional Standards link into the training and development of teachers, the individual, education providers, and the teachers and trainers within them. Each stakeholder has a role in the creation of an inclusive learning environment.

Stakeholders involved in creating an inclusive learning environment

Equality and diversity in the classroom

To understand how to promote equality and diversity we must understand some other important concepts: stereotyping, prejudice and discrimination.

- Stereotyping means grouping all people together based on one of their characteristics.

LO1

- **Prejudice** means making negative assumptions about an individual or group without prior knowledge of the people involved.

- **Discrimination** means directly or indirectly creating a barrier to learning and progress.

In a classroom, a teacher has a unique position of power. A teacher who has a particular prejudice about a person can abuse their position of power which would lead to discrimination against that person.

Power + Prejudice = Discrimination

> **Case Study**
>
> Joanne attended a course and was a model student, achieving the highest grade possible. She was voted class representative and went on to university to study further. Her sister Matilda starts the same course with the same teacher a year later. The teacher assumes that she will be the same as her sister – a model student who achieves high marks and goes to university.
>
> 1. Explain why the teacher is being prejudiced.
>
> 2. Describe three different ways in which Matilda might be discriminated against in this scenario.
>
> 3 Who else could be discriminated against in this scenario?
>
> As teachers, reflection on our own prejudices is essential to protect against indirect or direct discrimination.

In the Equality Act (2010) some different types of discrimination are described. Here are some examples:

- **Direct discrimination** – treating someone unfairly because of a protected characteristic – Example: No female toilets are available in the engineering centre.

- **Indirect discrimination** – creating a situation whereby someone with a protected characteristic is disadvantaged. Example: All exams are 3 hours long, provided on white paper, and answers need to be handwritten.

- **Harassment** – behaviour that is offensive or impacts on an individual's dignity and is associated with a protected characteristic. Example: Students using offensive language in the classroom and is not challenged by the teacher.

- **Victimisation** – the unfair treatment of someone who has made a complaint based on their experience with a protected characteristic. Example: A student complains through the college's procedures and is then ignored or treated harshly by the member of staff managing the class.

The Equality Act (2010) makes it illegal to discriminate against people based on protected characteristics. It ensures that education providers and teacher/trainers provide fair provision and make reasonable adjustments for individual learners based on protected characteristics and individual needs. Examples of its application might include:

- Ensuring a learner with mobility constraints can access the classroom easily without obstacles such as large furniture or bags on the floor.
- Access to prayer space and consideration of the impact of different religious events, such as fasting through Ramadan.
- Enabling all students access to courses that have a strong gender bias, such as Childcare and Bricklaying.

Ideas for teaching…promoting equality

Here are some more ideas of how we can promote equality in the classroom, based on the protected characteristics:

Protected characteristic	Positive action to create inclusive space
Age	Using various examples and images which highlight people of different ages in different careers.
Disability	Ensuring room layouts are accessible and welcoming for learners using a wheelchair.
	Creating lessons with individual learners' needs in mind.
Gender reassignment	Using the correct pronoun, as agreed with the learner.
Marriage and civil partnerships	Celebrating marriage and relationships in all their forms. Using examples within the news to discuss.
Pregnancy and maternity	Making reasonable adaptations as necessary to sessions and courses with a new or expectant mum.
Race	Considered approach to lesson creation, ensuring different images and examples are used to engage all learners within the classroom. For a learner to see an example of someone they identify with doing their dream job is empowering.
Religion or belief	Promoting celebrations of different religions and acknowledgement of their significance.
	Being interested and curious about the learner's experiences.
Sex	Being mindful of the common phrases we use for groups. "Okay guys….lads….girls….let's make a start." Unconsciously we are confirming that the group is made up of one gender.
Sexual orientation	Providing a safe and welcoming space for individuals to be open about their sexual orientation by the way we discuss examples in session. Equally, challenging homophobic comments within the session.
	In some cases this may be the first time they have been able to acknowledge it publicly.

LO1

> **Activity**
>
> Consider the nine protected characteristics in The Equality Act (2010). How can you ensure fairness of access and treatment in your education environment? Create your own list of positive actions to creating an inclusive space for education.
>
> | Protected characteristic | Positive action to create inclusive space |
> |---|---|
> | Age | |
> | Disability | |
> | Gender reassignment | |
> | Marriage and civil partnerships | |
> | Pregnancy and maternity | |
> | Race | |
> | Religion or belief | |
> | Sex | |
> | Sexual orientation | |

Examples of diversity

Whilst legislation ensures different characteristics are protected, the promotion of diversity celebrates those differences. Individual professionals and education organisations will look for ways to recognise and encourage differences, perhaps by showing support to Pride events, promoting STEM (Science Technology, Engineering and Mathematics) courses specifically to female students, and celebrating events such as Diwali.

Understanding your organisation's approach to diversity, equality and inclusion can offer inspiration and support to an early career teacher or trainer.

> **Case Study**
>
> September arrives and a teacher, Arnab, meets their new class for the first time as a group. Interviews have taken place during the year and information about prior attainment have been collated, but this is the first time the group has come together in a room.
>
> - What will Arnab need to consider before the group arrive?
> - What could he do initially to create a supportive and inclusive classroom?

> **equality** – the promotion of sameness in treatment
>
> **equity** – the promotion of fairness in treatment
>
> **diversity** – the variety of people in a class with differences in their background, experiences and lifestyles.
>
> **stereotyping** – grouping all people together based on one of their characteristics
>
> **discrimination** – directly or indirectly creating a barrier to learning and progress
>
> **prejudice** – making assumptions about an individual or group without prior knowledge of the people involved

> **Reflection Question**
>
> What are your experiences of equality and diversity?
>
> - Did you experience or witness unfair treatment in education or employment?
> - Why do you think equality and diversity are important in education?
> - What are your prejudices and how will you address them?

Ideas for teaching...promoting equality

Here are some specific ideas to promote equality and diversity:

Diverse pictures on the walls. E.g. People with protected characteristics working in vocational areas on the display boards.	Using laptops to set individual preferences. E.g. coloured screen, font style, voice recording.	Offer a range of diverse guest speakers.
Discover the wealth of IT learning support provided by apps, e.g.: • text-to-speech software • mind mapping software to cater for different learning styes	Diverse pictures and case studies used ad part of a teacher's delivery.	Using a variety of activities within a lesson, e.g. fill-in-the-gaps handouts, interactive learning, group work, quiet work, team activities.
Laying out the classroom for ease of access.	Addressing inappropriate language, initially as a teaching opportunity but always challenged and corrected.	Finding out about individual learners' life experiences through varied 'getting to know you' activities.

Ideas for teaching...equality and diversity

- Create a regular session to discuss what's happening in the news, particularly around discrimination and prejudice.
- Find some time for everyone in the class to find out about each other regularly - not just at the beginning of courses.
- Create case studies and activities that promote differences.
- Watch www.channel4.com/programmes/the-school-that-tried-to-end-racism with your classes and discuss privilege.
- Discuss the research of the 'Blue eyes, Brown eyes' experiment by Jane Elliott in 1968.
- Where there is an event – such as Pride, Diwali, Eid al-Fitr, Para-sports etc. – celebrate it with your groups.
- Watch the Rita Pierson TED Talk 'Every kid needs a champion'.
- Watch the Anindya Kundu TED Talk 'The boost students need to overcome obstacles'.

1.4 Explain why it is important to identify and meet individual learner needs

Understanding and knowing our learners as individuals provides the baseline for creating successful partnerships between teachers and learners. Mutual respect is built by understanding each other's expectations and learning about a student's past experiences.

There are many methods used to ascertain prior achievement and recognise any knowledge or skills gap. This process is important for any student on a new qualification. This section will introduce the role that initial and diagnostic assessments play in supporting learners and understanding their current position.

Abraham Maslow's Hierarchy of Needs (1943) is a good place to start when considering the needs of a learner and how as an organisation or teacher/trainer we can help meet those needs.

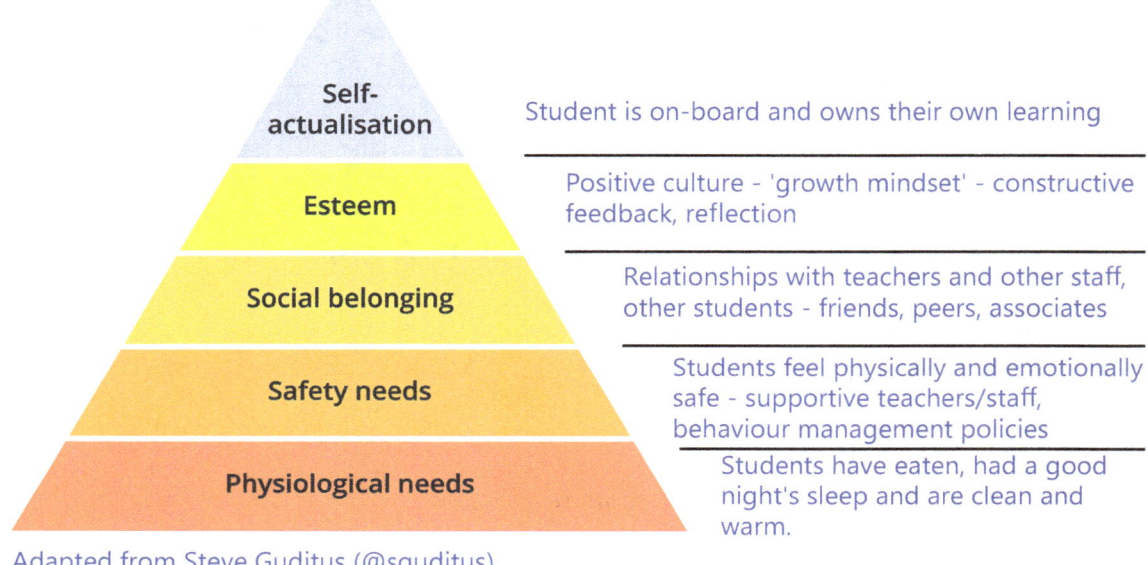

Adapted from Steve Guditus (@sguditus)

The theory behind the model is that individuals will reach their true potential at the highest point, called 'self-actualisation'.

- Firstly, basic levels of care need to be provided for such as food, water, shelter.
- Once these fundamentals are catered for the next stage is a sense of safety and security
- The next stages are love and belonging, and then self-esteem.

Only once these four levels have been met only then can "self-actualisation" occur.

In the diagram above we have considered Maslow's Hierarchy of Needs in the context of education. This can be considered at an organisational level and as well as at a teacher level.

> **Activity**
>
> Take some time to reflect on how you and your organisation support a student through their hierarchy of needs. Consider each stage of the hierarchy.
>
>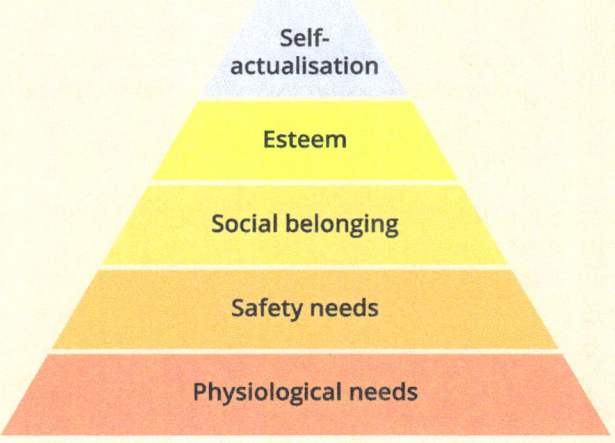

How do we identify learner needs?

Organisation level

Information gathering starts at application to a course by asking students to record:

- their prior attainment, such as previous qualifications and educational background
- any conditions that might need some additional educational support, such as dyslexia, dyscalculia, dyspraxia, autism, or ADHD
- any physical disabilities
- any mental health conditions.

It should be noted that these questions are sometimes not answered fully. Contact with the student at the beginning of the course can provide more enlightening information.

For learners aged 16–19 years there may also be some questions regarding their home situation, and whether they are a looked-after young person – i.e. living with foster carers or being cared for by a sibling.

Lastly, there may be some questions about finances if the course has a charge attached. Learners are often able to apply for bursaries to support them.

Generally, education providers will offer an interview, or at least an induction session, to ensure that learners understand the scope of the course they are about to embark on. Interviews are an ideal opportunity to get to know learners early on and understand their motivation for doing the course. This is often also repeated in the initial 'getting to know you' stage of any course or training session, allowing the teacher/trainer to be familiar with individuals' motivations.

LO1

Learners who are neurodiverse

Neurodiversity is the umbrella term for a broad range of behavioural traits. It encompasses the different ways in which people process information, the way they move, think or generally behave. It is not a single condition and quite often, different behaviours will be intertwined. Individuals are all different, and the way they learn depends on their previous experiences, their neurodiverse condition and how they process information. As a teacher, you need to be aware of neurodiversity and consider the teaching strategies that will support learners.

ADHD — Attention Deficit Hyperactivity Disorder is a learning and life condition which, according to ADHD Aware, is *"a group of behavioural symptoms that include inattentiveness, hyperactivity and impulsiveness. It is one of several different neurodiverse conditions including dyspraxia, dyslexia and autism including Asperger's."* www.ADHDAware.org.uk

Autism Spectrum Disorder — Autism is not a disease or illness; it means someone's brain works in a different way from other people. Diagnosis can be at any age as signs may be noticed when young or older. Each autistic learner will be different and have a different set of signs to another. The NHS website, alongside other specialist organisations, has some up-to-date resources on signs of autism, along with videos and resources that can both support individuals and raise awareness of the neurodiverse condition.

www.nhs.uk/conditions/autism/what-is-autism

www.autism.org.uk

Dyscalculia — A specific learning difficulty with mathematics, primarily arithmetic. It was defined in a UK Government document in 2001 as: *"Dyscalculia is a condition that affects the ability to acquire mathematical skills. Dyscalculic learners may have a difficulty understanding simple number concepts, lack an intuitive grasp of numbers, and have problems learning number facts and procedures. Even if they produce a correct answer or use a correct method, they may do so mechanically and without confidence."*

It is defined in the USA (Diagnostic and Statistical Manual of Mental Disorders, 2013) as: *"Difficulties in production or comprehension of quantities, numerical symbols, or basic arithmetic operations that are not consistent with the person's chronological age, educational opportunities, or intellectual abilities."*

Research into dyscalculia has lagged far behind research into dyslexia, but this is beginning to even out. Researchers agree that there is no single profile of dyscalculia. It is a diverse condition which is compounded by the range of demands in maths. Dyscalculia prevalence is at around 5% of the population. www.dyscalculiaassociation.uk

Dyslexia — A specific learning difficulty (SpLD) which primarily affects reading and writing skills. However, it does not only affect these skills. Dyslexia is actually about information processing. Dyslexic people may have difficulty processing and remembering information they see and hear, which can affect learning and the acquisition of literacy skills. Dyslexia can also impact on other areas, such as organisational skills. It is important to remember that there are positives to thinking differently. www.bdadyslexia.org.uk

Dyspraxia (developmental coordination disorder) — Dyspraxia in adults is a coordination disorder that affects movement, coordination and fine-motor skills, such as writing and working with small objects. Like the previous neurodiverse conditions, it does not affect intelligence but can affect balance and movement. It can also affect how one deals with emotions and social situations.

Credit to Elizabeth Wilkinson MBE – Dyslexia Dyslexic Consultant who has kindly contributed the definitions and supported on the writing of this section

Classroom level

Once courses are underway, the initial assessment stage of a program continues and allows teachers and trainers to gently assess the level their learners are working at.

- This can be through a written activity, set homework or a classroom practical activity.
- Within vocational education it can often be in the form of a 'trade test': chefs, for example, may be given a practical activity to show-off their prior knowledge and experience.

Whilst this can feel onerous to a nervous student, positivity from the teacher will enable learners to develop confidence and will provide clear information around the learner's needs for the course.

Individual level

Often learning styles are assessed to further support students. It is important to note, however, that as an educational tool, learning styles have been very strongly argued against.

> !!!!!! WARNING !!!!! WARNING !!!!!!
>
> Learning styles come with a WARNING! Learning styles are outdated and have not been favoured for a while and with good reason. Recent research and studies show that there is very little, if any, evidence that learning styles support teaching and learning strategies and that if anything, they can be potentially harmful to the learning experience. Coffield (2013) goes as far to say that there was no hard evidence to show that learning is improved using learning style questionnaires. Coffield et al. (2004) clearly questioned the benefit of determining individual learning styles as limited and limiting to learners. However, they are a tool at our disposal which can offer limited insights into the current status of our learners. As educational/training professionals there is every chance that you will come across them and, as a result, it is our duty to discuss them as opposed to sweeping them under the carpet.

A popular assessment of learner styles is the VAK questionnaire, which is meant to indicate whether a learner has a preference towards Visual (seeing), Auditory (hearing) or Kinaesthetic (doing), learning. This type of activity is interesting to undertake as a group. Reviewing the results as a group can help a teacher understand some of the preferences that the group may have. However, there is debate around the benefit and validity of assigning a single learning style to individuals. It is always better to use a variety of resources and activities to ensure that all learners are included and no one feels left out.

There are other models too. Honey and Mumford (1986) suggest students can be classified into four possible types of learners:

- activists – need information in short, quick, bite-sized chunks
- reflectors – need time to think about the new learning
- theorists – need to understand where this new learning has come from and how it builds on previous theories
- pragmatists – need to be able to test out new knowledge, preferably in a practical situation.

This information can provide insight into how an individual may process information and new learning.

A more detailed assessment of Honey & Mumford's approach is well worth further review. See the link in the next Activity box.

LO1

> **Activity**
>
> www.mint-hr.com/mumford/
>
> Take this Honey and Mumford test and see where you currently sit on their model of learning styles.
>
> - What does this mean for your teaching?
> - What benefit does this offer?
> - What are the potential pitfalls?

Knowing about how someone learns and what motivates them helps support the learning experience for the individual. It takes time to do this and, of course, no two learners are the same.

For trainers, prior internal information about individuals is unlikely to be provided as this could be a breach of data protection. So the use of questionnaires and activities, allowing learners to acknowledge prior learning experiences, may provide some information to support the trainee within sessions.

Finding out about a learner's motivation for enrolling on a course can be interesting for the teacher. This can be especially true for a trainer. For example, finding out that a trainee is on the course 'because their boss says they have to be' would be really useful information for the trainer. Rather than spending the morning wondering why we have a reluctant and belligerent trainee, the trainer can use further questions to find out why that learner's organisation feel they need the training. For example:

- Have they have done the course, or one like it, before? If so, their experience and knowledge could be used to support other learners new to the course.

- Is there is a gap in their experience, understanding or knowledge and they have a blind spot to it? In which case adopting careful questioning and a coaching approach might help them see how this course may make their job or role easier.

> The art of questioning within the education and training sector requires more thought than is often given credit for. Most people are familiar with open and closed questioning and understand what this means. However, for teaching, learning and assessment, more knowledge is required to prepare and ask relevant questions to the right student at the appropriate time. It goes beyond Rudyard Kipling's Six Honest Serving Men:
>
> "I keep six honest serving men, (they taught me all I knew). They are What and Why and When and How and Where and Who."

In the classroom

I use a simple form which asks learners to describe their:

- motivation for the course
- their wider skills and experiences
- their last formal training or learning experience
- anything else they would like me to know to help support them in the classroom.

An example of this form is below:

AET Award in Teaching and Learning Jane Owen		
Name: _____ Contact Number(s):_____		
Contact Email: _____		
Programme/Course: AET February – June		
Why you want to complete this qualification?	Details of your skills, prior experiences, interests & last taken qualifications.	Any Learning / Physical Difficulties you want me to know? Any ideas on your preferred ways of learning?
Tutor notes:		

> **Activity**
>
> Research different questioning techniques and games. www.teachertoolkit.co.uk/ is a good starting place.
>
> Search for 'questioning' to see some articles, templates, and real examples. Alternatively, look at:
>
> https://tinyurl.com/47xjump6
>
> ...for three simple strategies.

Learners can also help us by creating their own learning goals and targets. An individual's ownership of the process, and on-going measurement of progress against targets, are essential for this approach to work. Involvement and advice from a teacher or mentor may also be needed. This can be another very helpful tool to understand the needs that a learner self-identifies – although they may still have other needs which they are not aware of.

Goals and targets

Goals can be written using online tools or they can just be handwritten. Consideration of the SMART acronym is beneficial to setting targets and goals:

- **Specific** – Include detail and break down elements of a larger goal.
- **Measurable** – There should be a way to check the goal has been achieved.
- **Achievable** – Goals should not be too easy but not impossible either.
- **Relevant** – Will achieving the goal mean moving forward with the course or learning?
- **Timed** – There should be a clear timeframe for the goal.

An example of a smarter goal would be to complete a specific assignment criteria by a specific date. Or more explicitly:

- 'To complete criteria P1, by 13th January'
- 'To read and make notes on 3 articles relating to teaching by half term February'.

Ultimately, a discussion with the learner about their learning style, learning difficulties, prior experience in the classroom or training environment, and motivation for being on the course, are the starting points for how we, as teachers and trainers, can meet that need.

Activity

Which tools in this section were your already aware of and which are new to you? Write two lists as shown:

Tools you are aware of?	Tools new to you?

How do we meet learner needs?

So, now we have explored how to identify learners' needs, we need to use that information to support their studies. This topic is also covered later in Learning Outcome 3.3 of this unit.

The information gathered by the educational provider during application and enrolment may lead to strategic support being put in place.

- For example, if a learner discloses a learning condition such as dyslexia then the organisation's systems will signpost that additional help may be needed during exams, such as extra time, a reader and/or a scribe (someone to write down answers).

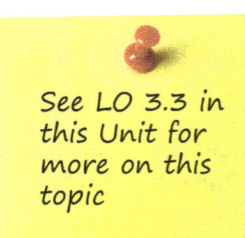

See LO 3.3 in this Unit for more on this topic

- For a looked-after young person a team of people, including a Safeguarding Lead, may be assigned to them to ensure they are supported in their learning. This information is also vital to the teacher in ensuring they individually support the learner, particularly in the early stages of their transition from school to FE.

Within the classroom, the teacher's knowledge of each learner's needs supports how they plan and consider the progress of a lesson. No one lesson will fit all, because within every cohort there are learners with a mixture of learning styles, abilities, and experience. However, planning lessons with consideration of all these different needs allows all learners to access the session and make it more likely they will enjoy their learning.

In practical terms, it can be difficult to accommodate all of the styles, all of the time. But awareness and acknowledgement of learners' preferences, within well-structured lessons, is often enough for learners to feel understood. In addition, the planning stage of lessons and Schemes of Work benefit from reflection on the learning sequence. What do learners need to know and understand before moving onto the next stage of learning?

Here some ideas about supporting learner needs, including neurodiverse learners.

> **Reflection Question**
> We have all probably experienced teaching or training that is not relevant, goes on too long, or run by a trainer that doesn't engage with us. How did that experience feel?

Learner need	Ways teachers/trainers can help learners
Dyslexia	To prevent visual stress, using coloured paper or overlays can support a learner with dyslexia. In my experience many people find reading on a coloured background easier than white. By offering the whole class coloured paper handouts we are supporting the individual – but the whole class benefits. Creating interactive and practical tasks within lessons, including student-led demonstrations, discussions, and presentations, can enable participants to showcase their knowledge and understanding more freely.
Dyscalculia	You should be aware of the fear that numbers can cause for some learners. Consider your questioning techniques where maths skills are required, to ensure learners don't revert to 'blind-panic' and not able to think about the maths-based question. Pose, Pause, Pounce (pose the question, pause for thinking, and pounce on someone to answer) is probably not the right approach. Whole-class answering at the same time may reduce the fear of getting it wrong. Group work, used effectively, can balance out the tendencies of individual learners, if you know which learners are more confident around maths-based activities.
ADHD	Be wary of using PowerPoint too much in lessons. PowerPoint can be useful as a prompt, and to provide a visual clue to the lesson. However, it is advisable to avoid covering slides in words to be copied or, worse still, listened to in entirety! Giving short, specific activities and instructions can keep attention from waning. Sometimes learners benefit from taking a walk or a short additional break to enable their concentration to come back to the lesson. This approach needs managing and supporting, depending on the maturity of the learner.

Looked after young person	Consider their access to IT support outside of the classroom when setting homework and assignment work. Movement between residences could cause difficulties with accessing IT and online support, and cause issues with attending college. Often providers have support mechanisms to overcome these issues, like the loan of laptops.
Learning preferences	Changing the pace of a session by mixing up activities will support all learners as the session progresses.

What difference does meeting these needs make?

Fundamentally, we are all individuals who like to be seen and heard. In a group setting, like a training session or classroom, we can feel ignored or not understood if our needs are not acknowledged or met. This can lead to poor behaviour and hinder our ability to learn, make progress, and achieve.

When you have learners with specific needs, discuss their support plan and ask what would help, but most importantly act upon it and be honest about what can and can't be actioned.

Identifying learners' needs	How might we meet their needs?	What is the impact?
Learning condition – Dyslexia, Dyspraxia, Dyscalculia, ADHD	Adapting learning strategies to provide equity within the classroom.	Learner feels accepted, understood, and supported. They are motivated to engage with learning.
Physical disability	Ensuring access to the classroom, the environment as a whole and the learning.	Learner feels welcomed and seen, and can access education.
Mental health condition	Providing institutional support, i.e. counsellors, classroom support. Acknowledging the challenges and providing options.	Initially, support can see a learner through a difficult stage. This support builds longer term trust in the teacher and organisation.
Home-life circumstances	Providing institutional support, i.e. mentors, pastoral tutors and through acknowledging the challenge and providing options. Practical support and advice such as setting up supported accommodation.	Referring back to Maslow's Hierarchy of Needs, supporting learners to ensure they have safe and secure accommodation is vital to their success in education.
Financial situation	From an organisational level this support may come in the form of bursaries, subsidised field trips and visits, or simply providing lunch tokens.	Again with reference to Maslow's Hierarchy of Needs, access to food is clearly linked to the success of a learner's day. Additionally, equality of access to field trips and even transport into school or college are a legal duty as well as a moral one.

LO2 Understand ways to maintain a safe and supportive learning environment

2.1 Explain ways to maintain a safe and supportive learning environment.

2.2 Explain why it is important to promote appropriate behaviour and respect for others.

2.1 Explain ways to maintain a safe and supportive learning environment

As already discussed, facilitating learning requires the learner to feel comfortable and safe in their environment. Drawing on Maslow's Hierarchy and meeting learning needs can significantly contribute to this. Additionally, safeguarding is a fundamental function of any education organisation with various laws and guidelines to ensure the appropriate protection of children and vulnerable adults. Refer to LO 1.2 for further details on the legal implications of safeguarding.

For this learning outcome we will focus on the practical approaches a teacher and organisation can take to ensure a safe and supportive environment for their learners.

There are two elements to maintaining a safe and supportive learning environment:

- the practical, physical elements of the rooms, the corridors, and the other communal spaces
- the atmosphere that is created through the teacher's management of the space, learning activities and interactions, as well as the culture within the organisation as a whole.

Maintaining a safe learning environment

An educational provider must adhere to the Health and Safety at Work Act by putting things in place such as:

- First Aid Provision: first aid kits, qualified first aiders, and in many cases defibrillators.
- Fire safety: safety officer, fire safety equipment, the organisation of fire evacuation drills.
- Invacuation drills – situations where learners and staff may need to stay within the building and classrooms.

Physical environment

The physical environment within a classroom includes:

- the layout, including the teacher area
- furniture and any other resources or items.

LO2

Layout

It is important to enable easy access to and around the room, particularly with learners who have mobility or sight impairments. You will need to consider:

- Space around tables.
- The arrangement of corridors between desks.
- Trip hazards.
- How easy it is to move the room around or create new spaces in the classroom.

A simple assessment of the room and layout can provide for a safer space for learners to access.

Possible alternate layouts include:

Layout	Positive aspects of this layout	Negative aspects of this layout
Paired Tables	Easy to achieve, aisles can be created to offer space for a wheelchair to access. Learners can focus on the front.	Learners may have to sit in the same seat each session. Not ideal for group work.
Group tables – commonly for four or six people	Wider aisles are created for access around the room. Good for group work and discussions. Easier to manage practical activities. The teacher/trainer can easily move around the room.	Depends on the size of the group and room as to whether this is feasible. Some learners will have their back to the front of the room.
U-Shaped	Allows for choice of seating if room has space to access all the way round. All learners can see one another.	Dependent on size of room and numbers of students. Void space in the middle of the room.

40

Many learners choose to bring in their own laptops to work on, which can lead to health and safety issues with charging cables laid around the room. Learners should understand that cables are a trip hazard, and teachers and trainers need to get into good habits to create safe spaces.

Information at interview and enrolment may indicate a learner who has particular needs regarding room layout. If so, this will require you to plan ahead and take a consistent approach throughout their time with you.

Furniture

Equipment and furniture in the classroom, and throughout the whole learning facility, should be in good condition and operate correctly. If the facility is well looked after it will feel safe to be there.

Within the classroom this may include:

- checking for broken furniture
- assessing any broken equipment
- checking the quality of other resources
- reporting broken lights or other nuisances.

It is also important to provide clear instructions to learners about:

Frayed or broken wires pose a significant threat and must be reported and replaced.

- where to leave bags
- ensuring there is safe space around bags and other possessions
- processes for leaving the classroom
- instructions for moving around the room – when they are and are not allowed to do so
- not moving furniture unless instructed to.

In terms of the wider learning environment the organisation has a responsibility to keep learners safe. This may involve:

- secure entry systems
- wearing of colour-coded lanyards
- ID badges.

These all help to ensure only students and permitted adults are allowed access. The organisation also has a responsibility to take due care and attention when employing people to work with children and vulnerable adults, following thorough vetting procedures for potential employees to ensure learners' safety within the environment.

Psychological environment

Safety can also refer to the atmosphere, culture, and the feeling of safety in a place. This should not be underestimated in its importance. With reference back to Maslow's Hierarchy of Needs, when learners feel safe they can thrive and learn well. If the opposite is true they may be just trying to survive the day, and learning can be compromised.

Within any organisation there are policies and procedures to guard against bullying and harassment. In an educational setting this is of vital significance. Whilst success depends upon the policies it also depends on the individual teacher's management of the group and the culture they create.

As a newly-qualified teacher or trainer, it is vital to understand your organisation's procedures for incidents of bullying and harassment. It is also important to:

- create an environment of mutual respect
- engage with individual learners to get to know them
- gain an awareness of what is happening in the room
- understand the experiences your learners are having outside of the room, which might indicate if they are feeling safe.

On a practical level the initial settling-in of a group can foster a sense of safety within the classroom. This is another reason why it is important to establish ground rules, mutually agreeing these at the beginning of a course. As the course progresses the focus should be on how the ground rules are implemented, and what happens if they are not.

Managing learner comments in the classroom can be a very simple but effective way to create a sense of safety within the room. Often seen as a joke, the impact of a derogatory comment on a less confident learner can be immense. A quick rebuke from the teacher could avoid any future comments; additional careful questioning, praise, and positive reinforcement to the receiver of the comment can build confidence and decrease the impact of such comments.

Cyberbullying describes bullying which takes place over the internet, when using smartphone messaging apps or social media platforms. Adults and children are equally at risk of negative comments but young people can be more susceptible as their world often revolves around social media and mobile phones. Strong guidelines around the use of mobile phones in classrooms can provide a brief break from the constant need to check their phones. Most adults tend not to have quite the same issues with their phones in class - however they may still fall foul of nasty comments and personal attacks that sometimes arise on social media.

The management of bullying and harassment links closely to safeguarding of learners and as such there is a legal duty of care. This duty of care is also assessed by external agents such as Ofsted. There is also an educational duty to create inclusive and accessible environments where all can learn safely.

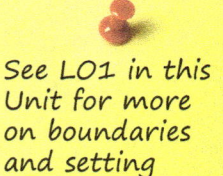

See LO1 in this Unit for more on boundaries and setting ground rules

Cyberbullying any bullying or abusive behaviour that takes place online

Quite often the teacher or trainer can be viewed as the trusted adult in the room, someone to rely on or confide in around issues that a learner is experiencing, and then offer sound advice and understanding of the procedures to protect the learner. Equally, the teacher or trainer is seen as a role model, and can be trusted to provide a safe space for a learner in the way they manage situations and address issues.

> **Activity**
>
> Consider the benefits and pitfalls of students using social media messaging platforms to communicate with each other outside the classroom.

Maintaining the supportive learning environment

A supportive learning environment offers the opportunity for people to thrive and develop.

There are a number of ways in which a teacher or trainer can encourage a supportive learning environment but all require initial planning and preparation to provide a consistent approach to teaching or training.

Lesson planning

Each lesson should be managed and structured to enable each learner to develop their knowledge and understanding of a subject from their own starting point. To do this, teachers need to plan their lessons. Creative lesson planning is an essential component in a teacher's toolkit. How do we get each learner on task when some already have knowledge and others have little?

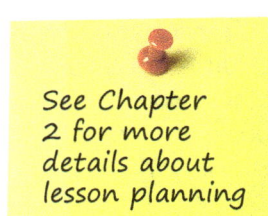

See Chapter 2 for more details about lesson planning

An example of a basic lesson plan format might look like this:

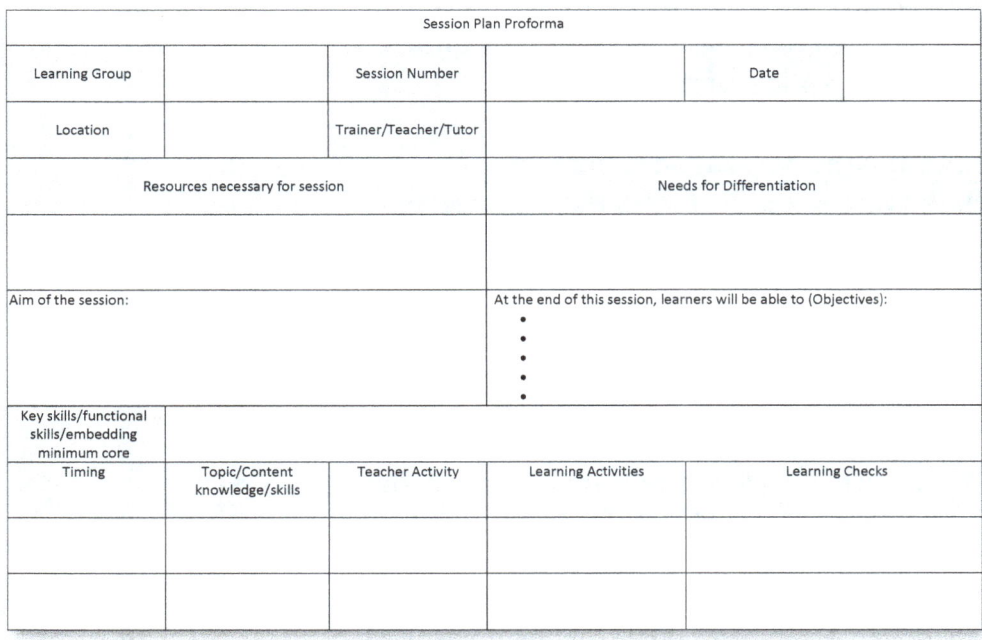

LO2

Lesson plans are built on the concepts of sequencing and differentiation.

Sequencing structures the learning process in a way which delivers for all learners.

"The curriculum in many subjects is dependent on a deliberate approach to the sequencing of knowledge because one concept often relies on the understanding of what has come previously and what will come next." (Howard and Hill, 2020, page 61).

In practice, sequencing means:

- Adding new learning to previous knowledge.
- Considering the starting point of all learners within a new course, topic, or section of learning. Some members of a class may have some knowledge where others have little, and so as teachers we need to ascertain where each individual is and ensure learning starts from a suitable point.

See Chapter 2 for more about sequencing lessons

Differentiation in the planning of teaching strategies allows learners at different levels to develop their knowledge and understanding in a lesson. It allows knowledgeable learners, and those with less understanding, to all feel that they are developing at their own pace. Homework and **flipped learning** tasks are useful tools here to support learners to develop their knowledge.

To find out more about flipped learning see flippedlearning.org

Further information on sequencing, differentiation and lesson plans will be covered in Chapter 2. Additional reading references are also given at the end of this section.

> ### In the classroom
>
> Considering a learner's previous knowledge is like asking them where countries are in the world and why people go to visit them. Some learners will have travelled, studied geography or history, and may have detailed knowledge of some locations and areas. Others may know about different places, and some may not know much at all. Teachers can use quizzes, games, and activities to encourage the 'knowledgeable' learner to share and deepen their knowledge by being the 'teacher' for the others.

Classroom management

The management of the classroom is covered by many excellent practitioners and resources. Recommendations for further research into this include: Paul Dix, Education Endowment Foundation, and The National College. As a new teacher or trainer, the ability to manage the classroom environment is a key skill in your toolkit to enable learner development.

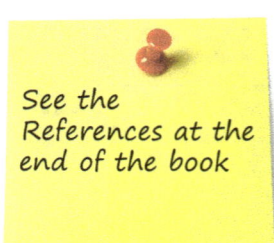

See the References at the end of the book

Management of the classroom is a very individual skill that does develop with experience. Some classroom management ideas that you could experiment with include:

- Creating a mutually respectful environment – welcoming and saying 'Good morning/afternoon' (and expecting a response!).

- Getting to know individual learners – their jobs, home situations, interests, and any issues they might have.

- Checking in with learners at the start or during a break in the session.

- Being thoroughly organised and prepared – this can feel overwhelming for each session in the initial stages of teaching but the resources you create now will hold you in good stead for the future. A good pace to a lesson doesn't allow poor behaviour to escalate.

- Getting regular feedback from learners and acting on it. Solution-based questions are often good, such as: 'List two things that are working within the lesson for you'. 'How could lessons be improved for you?'

- Using specific praise can be a valuable tool in gaining commitment to try new things with learners. Try to avoid generic phrases such as 'well done everyone'. Instead, aim for specific praise, such as: 'Laura, you have worked hard on that map, your key coding is very neat and clear, well done.'

- Praising effort rather than talent or results has been shown to develop a 'growth mindset'. Learners with a growth mindset are willing to try more difficult activities and not worry so much about failure. For more on growth mindsets, see Carol Dweck's TED talk.

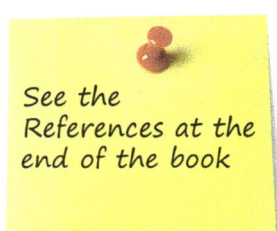

See the References at the end of the book

If a learner is not initially engaged with the learning consider why this is and use careful encouragement to ensure they understand the task. Is there something in their prior learning that is missing which means they are not able to do the task?

If a learner is consistently disruptive and not engaged, again, consider why this is. One option to resolve this is to take them from the learning space into a quieter space to have a one-to-one conversation. This can be the back of a large room, the corridor, or a staff room if appropriate. Sometimes this can wait until the end of the session, to avoid disruption to the learning, but sometimes it is needed in the moment. De-escalation of a situation, and an opportunity for people to better understand their behaviour and improve on this for future learning activities, should always be the goal.

If a learner is highly disruptive, intimidating other learners, or not allowing others to learn, a more drastic measure may be needed. On these occasions you may need to remove a learner from the classroom and ask them to come back at a specific time to discuss. In some cases, this may require support from the pastoral or leadership team to ensure the learner causes no issues whilst out of the classroom. Whilst rarely used, this approach is a necessary tool. However, it is imperative to understand what your organisation's expectation and approach is to discipline in the classroom.

In the classroom

My approach with disruptive learners is to be curious as opposed to confrontational. I might start the conversation with:

- 'I am wondering / concerned / worried about how you feel in the classroom. What is it that is stopping you from getting involved in the learning?' or
- 'Why do you think I have asked you to stay and talk to me?'
- 'How can I help you feel more confident about getting involved in the lesson?'

The block to learning is the starting point for a conversation, whatever the issue might be. Starting conversations from a place of wonder, provides an opportunity for the learner to be open and honest about how they are doing and feeling. It also offers an opportunity for them to recognise their roles and responsibilities in relation to their own learning and any choices they might make in the classroom.

In customer service I was trained to allow the customer to express their issues and complaints fully before offering solutions and actions. Jumping in too early can delay getting to the root of the problem. My approach to managing behaviour is similar. If I allow a learner, through curiosity and interest, to express how they feel in lesson, I am likely to understand more fully their issues and be able to offer support to resolve this.

In the classroom

In twenty years, I have experienced only one occasion when a learner refused to leave the room. This is often a question that arises when talking about classroom management with new teachers or trainers: What do you do in such a situation? In this particular example I asked the rest of the group to leave the room and wait in the corridor for me, and asked the learner who I needed to talk with to stay in the room. To say he was surprised was an understatement. I then explained to him that my experience suggests that young people do not like to have these types of conversations in front of their peers, and the reason for asking him to step outside for a conversation was to save his embarrassment! We quickly resolved the issues and I was able to allow the group back in to continue the session.

Sometimes simple actions such as managing the environment can offer quick wins for encouraging behaviour to aid learning. Early in a course or programme some options include:

- moving the classroom seating arrangements around regularly
- managing where people sit
- managing paired and group work to keep moving and mixing people around.

There are two main benefits to these strategies. Firstly, it avoids the cliques that can form. Secondly it allows the teacher to observe learners in different working partnerships. When managed quickly, in an organised way, and with a good pace to the lesson and activities, the reluctance and worry about working with new people is diminished. The more this happens in the classroom, the more of a 'norm' it becomes, and issues of disruption become less apparent.

Interestingly, in the post-lockdown classroom, a number of these techniques couldn't be used – learners had to sit in their normal seat and there was limited opportunity to mix people around the classroom. There has been a noticeable difference in learners not getting to know the whole of their learning group.

Finally, and possibly most simply, moving around the classroom whilst delivering a lesson, and whilst activities are ongoing, gives a clear signal to learners that it is as much the teacher's space as the learners'.

- Delivering content from the back of the room can ensure all learners hear your points.
- If low-level chattering is an issue, standing near the learner whilst continuing to deliver the content, often reduces their need to chat off-topic.
- Questioning directed to chatting learners or learners who appear distracted can be a simple method to reengage them.

Some other simple approaches to classroom management include:

- Use names to get attention – it is often the one word that any learner will hear through a myriad of other words and get them back with you.
- Use topic questions directed at people to keep them engaged and focused on the lesson.
- Wait for quiet before starting, and stop and start again if you are interrupted.
- Stop and stare if there is a disruption, wait for quiet before starting again.
- Create a signal that you are about to talk – using phrases such as 'Quiet please' or 'Listen in', repeated as needed. Used consistently, learners will come to know the signal.
- Move around the room, use the space.
- Remain calm and outwardly composed.

Activity

What methods will you use to manage a classroom?

List three strategies you already use or have observed and three new methods you are going to try.

LO2

Individual support

For learners who need additional support, it is important to understand how this support is useful to them. Conversations about what works and doesn't work will help these learners feel supported and understood. This is clearly linked to section 1.4 – review this for further detail.

Equally, when we are managing paired and group work, it is important to know what support individuals may need to ensure they feel confident in the pair or group they are allocated. We will discuss this in Chapter 2 when we review learning approaches.

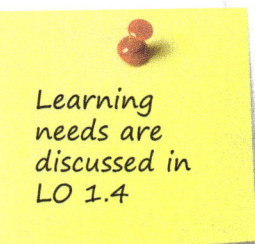

Learning needs are discussed in LO 1.4

Clearly, the way we negotiate ground rules is essential to individuals understanding expectations around their behaviour and their own responsibility in the classroom. This is also true of the way we manage those ground rules.

Ultimately it requires teachers to take a consistent approach for learners to feel confident and supported in their learning space. The way we start lessons, organise activities, and manage the room, all provide learners with signals of what to expect and what will happen next. A consistent approach and pattern of lessons can be especially important for learners with learning needs and helps to create a calm classroom for all.

Questioning techniques, which is often discussed in Continual Professional Development (CPD or 'on the job' training) sessions, considers not just the different ways we can pose questions to a group but also the use of 'Thinking Time' where the room may be quiet for a moment before someone is asked to answer. This allows learners who process information differently to respond. A good questioning technique also fosters a culture of having a go and not fearing failure. The way a teacher responds to an incorrect answer is key to building this confidence to have a go.

questioning techniques the art of choosing and asking questions that aim to assess the level of learning for individuals

'Pose, Pause, Bounce' is a recognised questioning strategy that, when used effectively and consistently, can give time to learners to consider answers and respond to the teacher/trainer's question. However, as stated previously, not all learners can cope with this method, so it is important to know your learners and their needs before using.

In the classroom

In academic writing the phrase 'behaviour for learning' is used to describe learner behaviour which allows learning to take place. This behaviour depends on the learner's relationship with themselves, with their classmates, with their teacher, and with the curriculum. Within my college environment we have created a 'fitness to study' approach, which is different to a disciplinary process and focuses on supporting learners to ensure they are able to learn. This could be putting in place pastoral support and key support people to help the learner with wider issues which are barriers to their learning.

Communication

How we communicate, welcome learners to the classroom, get to know learners, and how we challenge inappropriate behaviour all go towards setting expectations for behaviour for learning. Communication is not just about what we say, but the way we say things and, as importantly, how we listen and take note of learners. Are we listening to understand, rather than listening to respond? These are skills which will develop over time, but it is important to note that the clarity of our communication is a real tool in the box for the new teacher or trainer.

> "There are two kinds of people: those that listen and those that wait to speak."

As discussed earlier (when considering praise, our approach to classroom management, and supporting individual learners) the words we use have impact and consideration should be given to them. Reflective practice with a supportive colleague can be helpful to consider our approaches, particularly after a critical incident, in terms of how we can manage situations differently in the future.

Reflection Question
Considering classroom management and creating a safe and supportive learning environment, what practices are you already aware of and use? What do you want to research further and how will you do this?

2.2 Explain why it is important to promote appropriate behaviour and respect for others

Within training and educational settings, the norms of conduct are established using policies and procedures. These approaches allow learners to feel safe and secure. If we return to Maslow's Hierarchy of Needs (LO 1.3), we understand that without a level of safety and security a learner cannot progress towards improving their self-esteem and onto self-actualisation, where learning can most successfully take place. So, it is vital to ensure we promote appropriate behaviour in order to create a mutually respectful place.

Activity
Why do you think appropriate behaviour and respect is important?

So why is a teacher or trainer's promotion of appropriate behaviour and respect so important?

- The learners are unlikely to read the policies and procedures for themselves - they are most likely to understand the educational institution's rules by observing how members of staff behave.
- Some learners may find the language in the written-down rules hard to understand.
- Consistency is very important in the classroom. A teacher who behaves appropriately at all times will also behave consistently. A teacher who sometimes behaves below accepted standards may find it harder to maintain control in the classroom.
- Some learners may not have good role models outside the classroom. It is even more important for such learners that teachers can promote appropriate behaviour.

Establishing standards

Organisations create policies and procedures to support learners in their behaviour, such as:

- zero-tolerance to bullying and harassment
- disciplinary policies
- support approaches.

However, teachers need to model the behaviour we wish to see. Hence, professional standards and behaviour are essential not only in the classroom, but also around the campus or facility.

The core behaviour of valuing and being interested in the individual learner establishes trust. It also establishes a professional relationship based on mutual respect.

In practice, this means that as a teacher or trainer you should model appropriate behaviour and respect by:

- Always being courteous and polite.
- Talking to learners with respect.
- Using professional language.
- Using a positive tone and de-escalation strategies rather than using aggressive tones or actions.

Student responsibility

Within learning organisations there is some form of formal contract at the point a learner enrols. This could be a financial agreement for adult learners or simply a learning contract in the case of training provision or 16-19 provision.

In addition to this, a student and/or group contract are often created within courses so that each individual agrees to a code of behaviour linked to the ground rules. The learner then has a personal responsibility to adhere to these rules and any deviation can be discussed using the contract as a base point for behaviour.

Within classroom sessions there are opportunities to reiterate expectations when introducing activities such as student presentations, peer working and assessment, and peer feedback. Creating these regular opportunities will help students to understand their responsibilities when working with their peers and in the classroom. Team-building and leadership activities can be used effectively to build respect and promote positive behaviour.

Encouraging the individual learner to promote positive behaviour and respect not only creates a productive learning environment, but also develops learners' wider life and employability skills – for instance, managing challenging situations effectively in the future.

Activity

List five considerations for creating a safe and supportive learning environment and what impact they make on learners' experiences.

Creating and safe and supportive environment	Impact of this action on the learner?
1.	
2.	
3.	
4.	
5.	

Reflection Question

Understanding what contributes to a safe and supportive environment can make all the difference in an individual learner's journey. Consider a time where you have felt safe and supported in your development journey. What difference did it make to what you could achieve?

Case Study

Ben, a young learner, starts on a course and makes new friends. He shares his mobile phone number and joins a number of messenger groups to share course information and arrange social activities. As the course progresses there are disagreements within the group and one other learner makes public comments about Ben on social media and shares his mobile number on a social media post. Ben starts to receive calls from people he does not know and reads comments about him on social media groups he is not part of. Ben begins to feel uncomfortable in the public places around college and it has an impact on how comfortable he feels in the classroom.

Ben has a good relationship with his tutor and shares the situation with them. Ben feels he could handle it himself but the tutor explains the institution's safeguarding policy and the legal implications of sharing Ben's information. Ben's situation is passed to the safeguarding team. He and the other learners are interviewed. Because of the age of the learners, parents and guardians at home are contacted to ensure everyone understands the gravity and legality of sharing other people's information. The situation calms, Ben does need to change his mobile number, but otherwise is able to carry on his course and settle back into college life.

1. How do the organisational policies support Ben?

2. How does the tutor's approach support Ben?

3. What lessons might be learnt by the organisation or tutor to avoid this situation in the future?

LO3 Understand the relationships between teachers and other professionals in education and training

> 3.1 Explain how the teaching role involves working with other professionals.
>
> 3.2 Explain the boundaries between the teaching role and other professional roles.
>
> 3.3 Describe points of referral to meet the individual needs of learners.

As you may have already recognised, teaching or training is not a solo profession. Throughout the duration of your career, you will meet, interact with, and at times, rely on other professionals. In this section we will explore some of these key relationships and what the boundaries are. We will also consider how we can effectively signpost learners to key agencies that will in turn support them and help them progress.

3.1 Explain how the teaching role involves working with other professionals

The previous case study introduced interactions with other professionals. These interactions can vary in many different ways, and is one of the areas where we can see a distinct difference between teaching and training.

Working with others in a teaching role

Within a teaching role, working with other professionals can be a little mystifying until you have settled into your role and are clear about the requirements of your learners, colleagues, line manager, college/training provider and awarding bodies.

Safeguarding

You will need to know who the safeguarding team is within your organisation. Most educational establishments will have posters around showing who the team is and giving contact numbers. You will need to work with this team, so become familiar with their names and roles. Usually there will be mandatory training that will provide an overview of the process should you need to report an incident to the team. The training will include a summary of what is and isn't reportable.

Another source of information that can be used independently or in conjunction with your mandatory training is the Education & Training Foundation www.et-foundation.co.uk. The Education & Training Foundation is an excellent source of information full stop, but in this case offers advice, support and information on safeguarding and the Prevent strategy.

Other professionals

Other professionals you may need to liaise with include:

- **Estates team** – to check that rooms are set up and available as required, with the appropriate resources on hand.

- **IT Services** – IT equipment is used in many classrooms and lessons - knowing who to report any IT issues to is crucial.

- **Exams team** – this department ensures that learners are registered on the correct courses and for the right assessments; they are also responsible for claiming certificates from awarding bodies for each learner.

- **Line manager** – within an organisation your manager is an important person to provide support, guidance and discuss issues with.

- **Senior Leadership Team** – within an organisation the SLT are responsible for running the organisation and all the staff and learners that are part of it. You will benefit from understanding who in the SLT has responsibility for what.

- **Other people in your department** – to ensure that everyone involved in a learner's journey are aware of the needs of individuals, can support you and the learners and contribute to the quality of the provision.

- **Internal quality assurance** – colleagues in your organisation who verify marking and assessment decisions and procedures, to ensure that internal assessments are being carried out properly. These colleagues have received special training from an awarding body.

- **External quality assurance** – the awarding body will usually appoint an external assessor, who does not work in your organisation, to check on assessment decisions and the quality of teaching provision, and may wish to meet learners to establish the quality of their experience.

- **Awarding bodies** – most courses are designed and certificated by an awarding body. The awarding body defines the content of courses and how they are assessed. As well as the external quality assurance they may contact teachers directly with information about training, assessment procedures and new qualifications.

Activity

Identify the skills required to ensure you have effective relationships with the teams and individuals mentioned in the list above.

Working with others in a training role

Trainers working with or within an organisation are likely to have a different set of professionals to work with. These other professionals may include:

- teams or departments within the company they are providing training for
- human resource departments of external organisations
- teams or departments within the company they work for (if employed)
- line manager, colleagues, senior management (if employed).

Note: Some trainers are self-employed. They will not have colleagues but may belong to other informal networks, or have peers to whom they can go to for advice and support.

Trainers do not always deliver training that is accredited by an awarding body, but they may have relationships with other quality assurance bodies or individuals.

External organisations often pay directly for training. Hence they may have a greater focus on 'return on investment' (ROI) i.e. how they will benefit from the training sessions. In some cases they might evaluate improvements to their business that the training has made. Therefore, it is important for trainers to consider the outcomes required by the external organisation, and the other professionals they work with, before planning training, so that the training is delivered correctly. This also ensures that monitoring and evaluation of delivery, and any final conclusions, can be made fairly and accurately.

Skills when working with other professionals

To ensure that these relationships are formed from the outset, some of the key skills required will include:

- Effective communication skills to determine requirements.
- A clear understanding of the outcomes required by the organisation.
- An ability to collate information that can be analysed and reported on.
- Negotiation skills, to navigate where there may be tensions or specific requirements that have not been considered.
- Team-working to ensure stakeholders are involved in the process.

Activity

In small groups, or individually, draw a mind map with you in the centre and identify all of the key personnel you may need to liaise with in order to set up a day-long mandatory training event for 15 people in an external company.

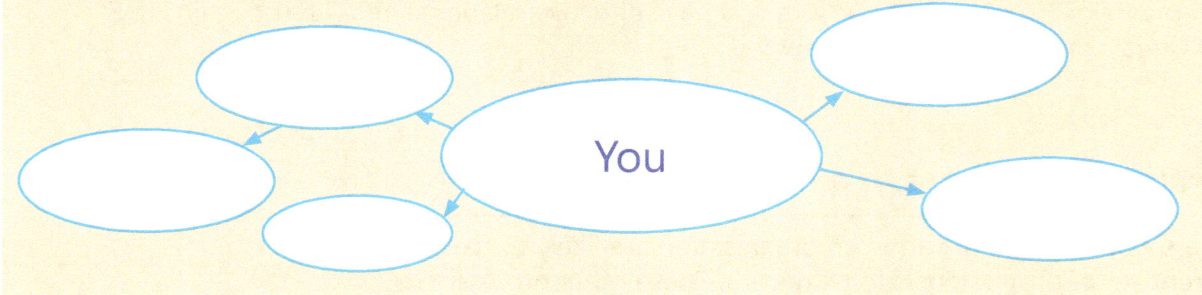

3.2 Explain the boundaries between the teaching role and other professional roles

Boundaries are the limits of something. In day-to-day life, a boundary often relates to a tangible item, such as the boundary of a piece of land. However, the boundaries in teaching roles and relationships are more difficult to clearly define than physical boundaries.

> **Activity**
>
> In order to help you prepare for setting boundaries with fellow professionals, take a moment to list the roles or job titles of the professional people you are in contact with on a daily, weekly or monthly basis. Consider the people within and outside of your organisation.

Identifying your role and responsibilities is crucial because this will help you to define the boundaries of your job role. Equally, part of the process of defining your own role and responsibilities will also help you to understand the roles and responsibilities of others. From this you can potentially identify where any gaps might be.

> **Activity**
>
> In the list of people identified in the activity above, now consider why you are in contact with them and in what capacity. How do they help you within your role and how do you help them?

> **Case Study**
>
> You have a learner who needs some help as she has just been made homeless and has nowhere to stay that night. The learner is aged 17 and will be taught by several tutors that day. You are her first tutor of the day, and she has shared with you that she had a serious argument with her parents who have asked her to leave immediately. As a result, she is homeless.
>
> - What should you do?
> - Who would you contact?
> - Whose responsibility is it to find accommodation for the student?
> - What are your responsibilities in this situation?
> - Can you identify any gaps?
>
>
>
> From your answers you will have identified the key people you need to communicate with to alert them to the learner's situation. You will have also identified whose responsibility it is to ensure she is safe. These professionals will also have roles and responsibilities. Where are the boundaries – who does what? And perhaps more importantly, who is expected to do what?

Boundaries can be ambiguous. Quite often, it is not until an important situation arises that we start to clearly define those boundaries and identify roles and responsibilities. In this situation, boundaries are about knowing who is expected to do what and ensuring that these responsibilities are completed. Effective communication is needed so that all involved are clear about the expectations and the outcomes. In the previous case study this may mean that you are allocated as the main communicating party, who ensures the learner is aware of the steps being taken to secure her safe accommodation.

> **In the classroom**
>
> Occasionally boundaries will change depending on the need. Once, on a trip with students, weather conditions had taken a very sharp turn for the worse by the time we returned home. Snow and blizzards delayed our expected arrival time and meant that some students were unable to get home that night. As a result, we booked taxis and overnight accommodation for the stranded students until they could return home safely. Usually, this would be done by different people within the educational setting, but in this instance, the situation dictated that action needed to be taken immediately, and in accordance with the student needs, by individuals who usually would not normally be involved in this process.

3.3 Describe points of referral to meet the individual needs of learners

Not only do we need to know who does what and when, we also need to be 'signposts' to other professionals and services as the need arises. Whilst a teacher or trainer does not need to be the source of all knowledge, you will be expected to have a general awareness of the services provided by your organisation – or at least know who to refer to if you need more information. The pastoral aspect of the role will often require further knowledge of the pastoral services available within your setting.

Expect the unexpected. Questions you may be asked, or advice that may be sought can range from what steps should the individual take next to what financial support is available to them and anything inbetween. You don't need to have all the answers, but you may want to help answer the question by referring the individual to another team or agency.

As well as dealing with questions, we need to know who to speak to and what to do in a range of scenarios. For instance:

- You may suspect a learner is being subjected to bullying, domestic abuse or neglect. These are serious concerns which you would need to refer to the safeguarding team immediately.

- You may suspect a learner of plagiarism, collusion or other forms of academic malpractice. This would be addressed through guidance from the exams team and awarding body.

- Occasionally learners will demonstrate serious behavioural issues or specific learning needs that need to be addressed and managed. Other professionals in your organisation may be better placed to deal with these situations and should be consulted. An understanding of the support available for both you and the learner is key. If you are not sure you should speak to your line manager or a member of the Senior Leadership Team.

The situations are not exhaustive, and there are many others that may come up. Understanding your organisation's policies and procedures will provide guidance on all these matters.

Activity

Research a real teaching or training job description.

Consider the role and responsibilities of the job. Which other professionals would someone in this job need to liaise with, to ensure they are as effective as possible?

We have now completed Chapter 1, in which we have explored the roles and responsibilities of a teacher/trainer. Please review the content of the chapter, identifying any gaps in knowledge or skills, and consider how you are going to take the development of these areas forward, using the action plan below.

What?	Why?	When?
What action is needed next?	How will this contribute to my development?	What is the timescale?

Chapter 2 Understand and using inclusive teaching and learning approaches in education and training

By the end of this chapter you will understand how to use teaching and learning theories in the planning and preparation of the microteach. You will also understand how these skills and methods are essential in developing lessons and training sessions that are part of a longer programme of study.

You will gain ideas for ways to create motivational and engaging learning, create an inclusive learning environment, and design, plan, deliver, and evaluate lessons. The practical application within this chapter will support you in choosing the topic for your microteach, creating suitable resources, and deciding on assessment methods to check learning.

Finally, this chapter will introduce you to reflective practice as an educator and consider how to evaluate sessions so you can be aware of your strengths, and the areas of your practice that you can develop. This will be supported by understanding how to give and receive effective feedback.

> LO1: Understand inclusive teaching and learning approaches in education.
>
> LO2: Understand ways to create an inclusive teaching and learning environment.
>
> LO3: Be able to plan inclusive teaching and learning.
>
> LO4: Be able to deliver inclusive teaching and learning.
>
> LO5: Be able to evaluate the delivery of inclusive teaching and learning.

LO1 Understanding inclusive teaching and learning approaches in education and training

1.1 Describe features of inclusive teaching and learning approaches in education and training.

1.2 Compare the strengths and limitations of teaching and learning approaches used in own area of specialism in relation to meeting individual learner needs.

1.3 Explain why it is important to provide opportunities for learners to develop their English, mathematics, ICT and wider skills.

1.1 Describe features of inclusive teaching and learning approaches in education and training

Within this section we will consider the approaches we can use to create an inclusive session, where all learners feel engaged and motivated. These sessions may form part of a broader curriculum, a qualification, a plan for a complete unit called a Scheme of Work, or a work-based training course.

In all cases the learning is broken down into manageable sections and learning is supported by scaffolding new ideas with established knowledge or skills.

Below are some of the main features of inclusive teaching and learning.

Equality of opportunity

As we discussed in Chapter 1, it is important to ensure the lessons we create provide opportunity for all participants to learn. In order to do this you will need to make sure all of your sessions are:

Accessible
Is there anyone within your group who needs information provided in a different way? For example,

- on their laptop prior to the lesson
- on coloured paper (to support visual stress)
- prepared materials available beforehand.

Also, consider the space and room layout to support access to and around the room, tables and seating, available visuals etc.

Differentiated
Activities should support different learning styles and levels of prior knowledge, for example:

- scaffolded activities which build on foundational knowledge for those who need support
- stretch and challenge activities for those who have developed their learning and need more stimulation.

Student-centred and student-led
Evidence shows that the more learners are involved in the act of learning, the more they will achieve and retain. Therefore, we need to create sessions where the learner is active, engaged and at the centre of their learning.

Meeting individual needs
We need to know our learners, and then use this knowledge when creating activities and lesson plans. This will help to ensure that each learner's progress is central to the planned session.

Varied learning styles
When planning sessions we should consider a range of different activities which support listening, seeing, and doing. For example, for some learners using an image at the same time as a written or spoken explanation helps them remember information.

Lesson planning
To make sure all of the elements listed above are included in each session, we need to plan lessons carefully. This preparation also gives a sense of organisation and confidence to the classroom and the teacher or trainer.

There are many top tips on how to prepare lessons and you will find the structure that works for you over time. However, it is important to stress the significance of the time you give to planning and preparation of your lesson.

The creation of an inclusive learning environment, and the planning and preparation of the lesson, are key to the assessment of the microteach element of the Award in Education and Training.

> "Tell me and I forget.
>
> Teach me and I may remember.
>
> Involve me and I learn."
>
> Benjamin Franklin

Active and passive learning

It can be helpful to plan for both active and passive learning. (These terms refer to the involvement of the learner – not the movement of teacher!)

Active learning is where the brain has to problem-solve and critically think in order to deepen knowledge.

Passive learning is where the brain absorbs information to build understanding – for example reading this chapter is an example of passive learning.

The diagram opposite is Edgar Dale's 'Cone of Experience' (Dale, 1969) which demonstrates how different activities influence how much we remember. In this model the focus is on remembering information. Dale proposed eleven levels of experience that move from concrete learning experiences through to more abstract experiences. From the diagram, you will see that these experiences are focused on the various types of media that can be used. However, understanding goes further than simply remembering the fact. We will discuss this when we investigate Bloom's Taxonomy in Learning Outcome 3 of this chapter.

See LO3 and the Appendices for more on Bloom's Taxonomy.

The Cone of Experience (Dale 1969)

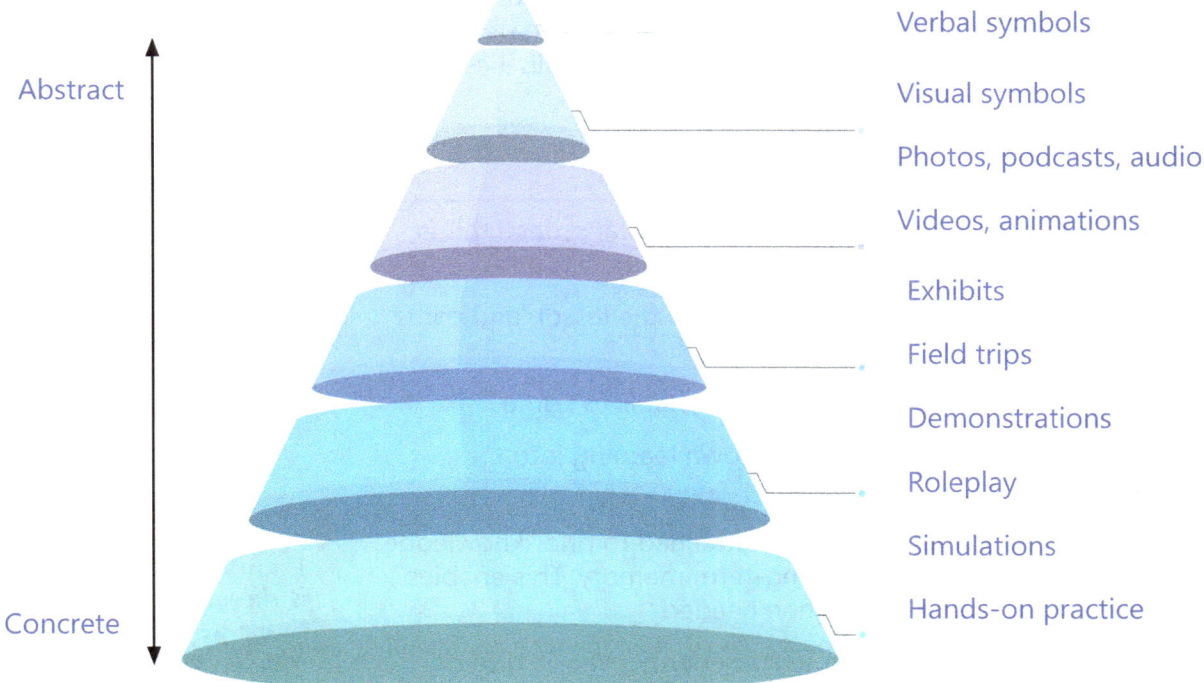

Abstract ↕ Concrete

- Verbal symbols
- Visual symbols
- Photos, podcasts, audio
- Videos, animations
- Exhibits
- Field trips
- Demonstrations
- Roleplay
- Simulations
- Hands-on practice

Edgar Dale (1969)

The passive learning (Abstract) section of a lesson is important as it helps set the scene of the session. There was a time when lessons mainly consisted of reading text, and people still progressed and learned. However, it is the application of learning (Concrete) which really brings learning to life.

During the Covid pandemic there was a need to return to quite traditional teaching methods, including static seating arrangements. These methods limited active learning, such as group work, and had an impact on engagement and involvement in learning.

Example in Practice

A group of Travel and Tourism learners need to know about tourist attractions that motivate people to visit South America.

Passive (abstract) learning: Learners could be asked to research landmarks in South America including: reading brochures, guide books, magazine articles and trade articles. Learners could access online video promotion films for South America to support their knowledge.

Active (Concrete) learning: Learners could be asked to work in groups to discuss their research and then decide on five landmarks that represent the variety of attractions that South America has to offer. They could then be asked to create promotional material for their landmarks, including a video, a guide leaflet, and a presentation.

By using the cone of experience as a structural guide we can support students to build knowledge and then apply it to an activity, which can be assessed.

LO1

When planning subject-specific lessons, some learning goals will lean more towards passive or active learning. But by bringing both methods together to produce meaningful lessons, learners will not only remember information but understand it. This approach can be used for theoretical or academic learning, as well as practical skills-based learning.

Structure

Lessons and schemes of work should come in a logical order - this is referred to as sequencing. Sequencing is important because it:

- enables learners to know what comes next in the lesson and come prepared
- relaxes learners because they understand what is to come
- creates a logical structure that breaks down learning into manageable chunks.

Each element of new learning needs to be attached to prior knowledge and linked to prior experience in the long-term memory. This enables learners to retrieve this information when needed.

Sequencing lessons properly takes time and energy. We will discuss planning lessons in detail in LO3 later in this chapter. However, one approach to consider now is Bradley Lightbody's Diamond Lesson plan:

Planning lessons is discussed in more detail in LO3 of this chapter

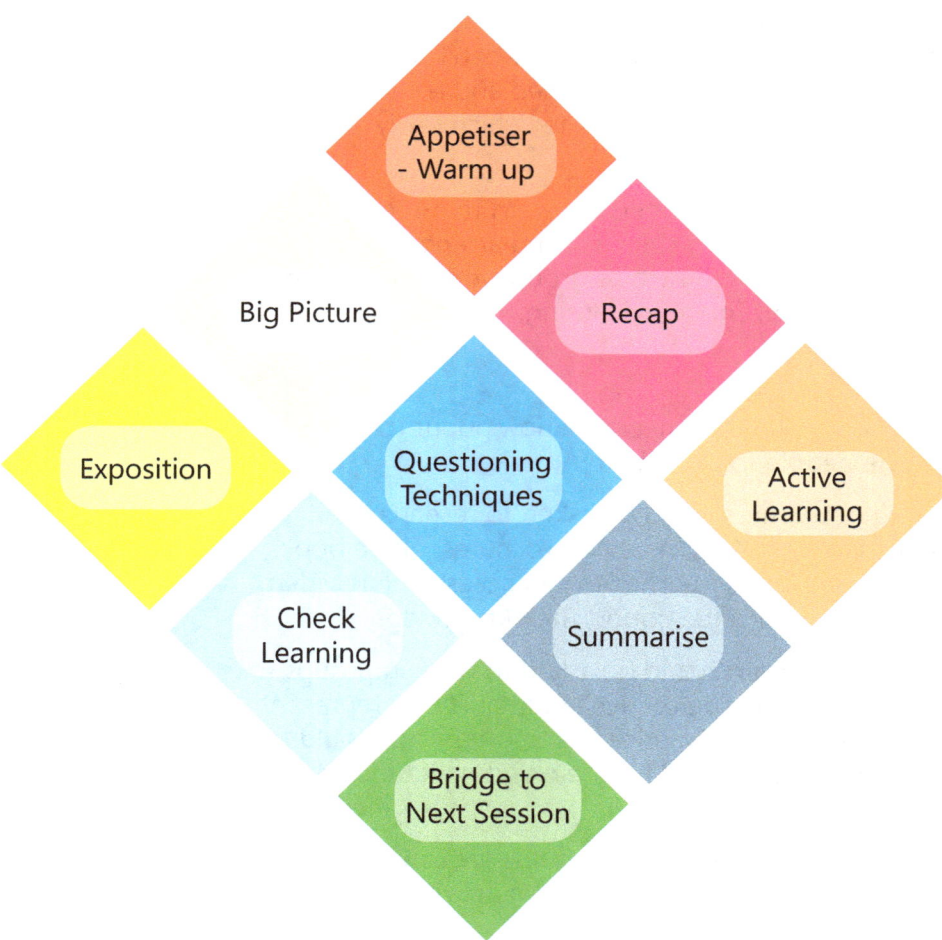

The following questions are linked to the stages of the Diamond Lesson plan and may help clarify the structure and chunks of the lessons:

- **Appetiser - Warm up:** How will I introduce this idea, concept, new topic?

- **Big Picture:** Can I create a story-type question or statement, to bring learners into the picture quickly and at an emotional level?

- **Recap:** What retrieval activities will I use?

- **Exposition:** How will I break this learning into manageable, logical chunks?

- **Questioning Techniques:** What questioning techniques will I use?

- **Active Learning:** How will I set individual, paired and group work?

- **Check Learning:** How will I check understanding throughout the session? What assessment for learning activities can I develop?

- **Summarise:** Is there an assessment strategy that allows learners to have immediate feedback, delayed feedback, self-determined feedback and teacher verbal feedback?

- **Bridge to Next Session:** How will I set meaningful homework that links to the next session?

Activity

Using one aspect of the Diamond Lesson Plan, create an activity that involves all learners that will address that heading. Consider the benefits of this activity for you and for the learners. Also consider the limitations and how you can overcome or address them.

Reflection

How will you make your session as interactive and engaging as possible for all learners? How will you avoid the trap of 'telling' the learners rather than 'teaching' them?

LO1

1.2 Compare the strengths and limitations of teaching and learning approaches used in own area of specialism in relation to meeting individual learner needs

To effectively compare the strengths and limitations of teaching and learning approaches, it is important to identify the strategies that could be used. In the table that follows, some strategies have been listed with potential strengths and limitations discussed. Neither the list of activities or the strengths and limitations are exhaustive. However, this table gives a format in which you can start to consider the activities that you use, and how they will benefit you and the learner.

Activity

Review the table opposite and add new activities to your lesson plan for the microteach.

Reflection

What teaching and learning approaches do you prefer to be taught with? Why is this?

	For the teacher		For the learner	
Activity	Strengths	Limitations	Strengths	Limitations
Teacher set and learner led - Group Discussion	New ideas. Peer engagement. Unusual answers. Time to explore wider ideas.	Risk of digression in discussion. Not able to answer the question. Going off on a tangent.	Allows **all** to engage. Can ask questions in a smaller group.	Some learners can dominate.
Teacher explaining through presentation	Sets clear information about the topic.	If long or complicated, difficult to keep all learners engaged and difficult to check understanding.	Record clear and accurate notes.	It is difficult to ask questions or clarify if anything is misunderstood. Passive learning.
Learners creating and delivering a presentation on a topic (individual, paired or groups)	Learners' own research leads to wider topics covered. Assessment of understanding (broader).	Risk of digression from content needs. Group work can create tension. Some learners aren't confident presenting to peers.	Engagement in research and creating a presentation. Deeper understanding of topic presented – active learning.	May misunderstand the topic. Lack of confidence may limit the learner.
Teacher sharing a video	Can offer a visually engaging explanation of a topic.	May not hit the point, sometimes too long, learners can disengage.	Brings a topic to life. Gives space to think.	Disengaged and zoned out. Passive learning.
Learners completing independent research	Wider understanding of the topic.	Needs checking for accuracy.	Find own connections to topic. Active learning.	Go off on tangent of irrelevant research.
Teacher demonstration	Accurate approach to a skill in steps.	Can be slow and will need repeating.	Observe the skill being completed correctly.	May need slower steps and time to practice between steps.
Learning-by-doing, practising a skill	Observe skill in action to assess.	Difficult to observe everyone.	Builds confidence in ability.	Demotivating if too difficult.
Teacher setting individually directed study activities	Specific task related to the topic.	Harder to mark.	Become an expert in the topic.	Difficult if a learner misunderstands the task or topic.

1.3 Explain why it is important to provide opportunities for learners to develop their English, mathematics, ICT and wider skills

English (literacy), maths (numeracy) and ICT (Information and Communication Technology) are particularly important subjects. They form a significant part of the government's agenda, because they are important for the jobs market and wider economy.

- Literacy is important because all qualifications, courses and jobs require learners to read and write. Those with lower literacy abilities will find their main qualification harder, and could impact the future careers that are available to them.

- Numeracy is important because numbers are used to some extent in many courses, qualifications and jobs. For example, knowing how to calculate average marks in tests. Numeracy also encourages logical thinking and develops analytical skills, which are advantageous in most qualifications and careers.

- ICT is important because technology is widely used in all aspects of education and the wider world. People with limited ICT skills are at a disadvantage, because it will take them longer to achieve tasks that require the use of technology – for example, writing a PowerPoint presentation.

Practice and improvements in these skills have clear links to learners achieving their academic and career goals, such as passing a course or qualification, getting a new job or being promoted. It also leads to higher self-esteem and personal development.

All of these skills are essential to ensure people are employable. One of the challenges that the UK faces is that there are too many adults with low literacy and numeracy skills. This stifles innovation and economic development, and reduces social mobility. As our society becomes increasingly technologically complex, how can you train people to do jobs of the future that do not yet exist? You can't – but people with good literacy and numeracy have a better chance of working their way through a changing job market in the future.

It is for these reasons that the government insist that young people continue to study literacy and numeracy qualifications if they did not achieve good GCSE results in the subjects at the age of 16.

Equally, development in wider life skills are also very important. Examples of these life skills include:

- communication skills
- social skills
- self-management skills
- problem-solving skills
- creative thinking
- working in a team.

These skills are recognised as important. They will help students now and in the future, and can lead to promotions, progression, and improved social mobility.

These skills can be embedded within specific subjects. For example:

Subject	ICT	Maths	English	Wider skills
Plumbing	Creating a professional quote in Word, calculate the quote using Excel.	Pricing a job including cost of materials and time.	Using a professional format and structure to create a formal quote.	Leading a team to complete a job.
Hairdressing	Creating a price list and marketing material using Word and Canva.	Calculating ratios for measuring colouring chemicals.	Writing content for an accurate website.	Being salon manager for the day.
Health & Social Care	Writing up a research report.	Using data charts to predict trends in H&SC. Recording data using measuring equipment for nursing.	Creating an accurate and relevant report on a topic specific to H&SC. Reading reports and articles on the subject.	Being part of a team to complete a industry-relevant activity.
Sport	Creating a fitness programme using Word for a client to follow online. Create support videos for certain exercises.	Recording data from fitness testing, and comparing it to previous test results.	Reading reports and articles to create a summary of information.	Leading a coaching session in order to demonstrate leadership skills.

Activity

Create a list of the activities which could improve learners' English, maths, ICT and wider skills within your area of teaching.

Reflection

What difference do you think wider skills make to learners in your teaching or training area?

LO2 Understand ways to create an inclusive teaching and learning environment

2.1 Explain why it is important to create an inclusive teaching and learning environment.

2.2 Explain why it is important to select teaching and learning approaches, resources and assessment methods to meet individual learner needs.

2.3 Explain ways to engage and motivate learners.

2.4 Summarise ways to establish ground rules with learners.

2.1 Explain why it is important to create an inclusive teaching and learning environment.

Why is an inclusive teaching and learning environment important?

Because it encourages learning

- **How might we achieve this?** By creating a safe space for learners to develop their knowledge and skills. This means creating a space where it is okay to make mistakes. A key element to understanding new knowledge is to get it wrong and then understand why that element is wrong and what would make it right. This has far more value than getting an answer right but not understanding why it is right.

> **Key tip**
> As a role model you create the space and sense of belonging in the way you get to know your learners and then use that knowledge to develop their feeling of safety and security to enable them to learn.

As a teacher you can model this approach by:

* valuing the differences and diversity in the classroom,

* by asking for advice and help with spelling on the whiteboard,

* by being authentic with what you know and what you don't know.

This creates a feeling of safety and security in the classroom and enables learners to become open to having a go and trying even if they are not 100% sure they will get it right first time.

Because it means that everyone in the room feels safe and able to participate

- **How might we achieve this?** We can challenge behaviour which would undermine the feeling of safety. This could be anti-social behaviour, disruptive behaviour, or discriminatory behaviour. There are many books written on classroom and behaviour management for teachers. (There is more on this in Chapter 1, and at the end of the book we have provided references for further reading.) Setting ground rules underpins classroom management, creating the safe environment required for learning. These rules are bought into by all and role-modelled by teachers.

> **Key tip**
> Remember how important it is to create a safe space for learners in your sessions. Not only will they learn the criteria for their assessments but they will also develop broader life and employment skills.

Creating a safe space for learning has further benefits, such as ensuring that learning opportunities are maximised because disruption is minimised, and ensuring learners know the pattern of the lesson and take responsibility to be ready to learn. This makes sessions more meaningful and impactful, and helps learners feel socially, emotionally, and academically accepted.

So that learners feel able to support each other

- **How might we achieve this?** By encouraging learners to work as a team within the classroom. This positive behaviour helps develop wider employment and life skills. By encouraging learners to help each other, we are also encouraging them to take greater responsibility for their own learning.

To develop independent learners who are more likely to deepen their skills and knowledge

- **How might we achieve this?** Setting homework tasks, encouraging, patterns of behaviour at the beginning of the session (like getting out pen, paper, and previous notes), and keeping to deadlines for assignments and exam revision – these all help to create independent learners.

Ideas for teaching...
'Getting to know ...' activities are a great way to settle people into feeling comfortable with their peers. Some ideas are:

- Introduce your partner – Interviewing and then introducing someone else is less pressured than introducing yourself.

- Human Bingo – Provide a bingo sheet containing facts about potential classmates, e.g. 'left-handed', 'owns a dog', 'has been to a concert in the last month', etc. Instruct students to find people who match the statements and sign in their box. Shout out 'Bingo!' when all boxes are complete.

> **Reflection**
> How will you use knowledge of your learners to engage them in the classroom and ensure they feel safe enough to make mistakes and develop their learning holistically?

LO2

2.2 Explain why it is important to select teaching and learning approaches, resources and assessment methods to meet individual learner needs

In Chapter 1 we discussed why it is important to identify and meet learners' needs. We also touched on ways in which we could meet various needs.

To meet the needs of different learners we can use:

- different teaching and learning approaches
- a range of resources
- various assessment methods.

This is important for the following reasons:

Why should we use different teaching and learning approaches, assessments and resources?

- *Because learners are likely to get bored if each lesson is exactly the same all the way through*

Planning sessions with a selection of activities, variations within the session and variations across a scheme of work, ensures each session is engaging. This helps learners to remain motivated.

- *Because some learners will be less able to access some resources*

For example, someone with a learning need may find certain fonts and certain colours hard to read. These learners would be at a disadvantage if only resources using these fonts and colours were available.

- *Because different people learn in different ways*

We can sequence learning to meet individuals' needs. This ensures that each learner builds up sufficient understanding to be able to approach the next stage of each lesson. To do this we would need to scaffold activities for some learners. **Scaffolding** means creating supporting elements for activities which meet the individual learner needs. In practice this might mean offering slightly different activities for different people within the session. This ensures all learners meet the outcomes by the end but with different levels of support.

These choices are also made to ensure that the sessions are suitable for the size and diversity of the group, with a balance of activities which engage them in learning that is relevant to their background and understanding. Creating this balanced approach to the sessions, incorporating different learning activities, will promote the learning process and stimulate learners to actively engage.

What are the different assessment methods?

Formative assessment can be defined as ongoing assessment, where learning and progression is checked as the lesson is taking place.

Formative assessment activities are designed to assess where learners are in their learning journey. Good formative assessment activities will highlight any gaps in knowledge and where they have good knowledge and understanding. Formative assessment directs the teacher to revisit areas where there are misunderstandings or lower achievement. Pages 104-105 have some more information on formative assessment methods.

Formative assessment activities support learning, and with structured repetition they move knowledge into long term memory. Timely structured repetition is needed to develop the retrieval of knowledge and form long term memories.

Summative assessment is the final outcome of learning. It checks a learner's knowledge and/or skills at a suitable end point and normally results in a grade, which can be used as a benchmark to compare different learners. It is often in the form of an exam, a test or an assignment.

When selecting teaching and learning approaches, resources, and assessment methods it is important to ensure they are appropriate to the level of the course, as well as to the learner's own level of skill and knowledge. As part of the scheme of work, which breaks down the topic or course into weekly sessions, the progress of the sessions will be clear; keeping to this schedule will meet the end results for the course.

> **Reflection**
> What will you take from this section to develop your microteach?

> **Activity**
> Research 'formative assessment methods' on the internet and create a folder of ideas for methods you could use.

2.3 Explain ways to engage and motivate learners

Much has been written about motivation in the classroom. In this section we will mainly discuss the practical methods to create engagement in the classroom. Initially though, one theory worth considering is 'Autonomous motivation' by Deci and Ryan (2008).

They highlighted three elements that need to be in place for a learner to feel 'autonomous motivation' in the classroom. Autonomous motivation comes from within and is when the individual chooses to engage with the teacher and within the lesson.

The three elements in this theory are as follows:

Autonomy	Competence	Relatedness
Learners to have some sense of choice and control within the classroom situation	*Learners to have some level of ability and knowledge within the subject being taught*	*A sense that learners belong and are known in the classroom*

Deci and Ryan (2008)

We can use this model when we plan our sessions and scheme of work, by:

- including variety and choices within the activities
- creating sessions which build on learners' prior knowledge
- getting to know learners and helping them to create a team within the classroom.

All of this will underpin the sense of motivation for the group and as individuals.

Clear outcomes

Considerations for engagement and motivation include setting clear outcomes for the lesson and for a group of lessons, so that learners understand why an activity is relevant and where it fits into the bigger picture.

Bloom's Taxonomy

Bloom's Taxonomy supports teachers and trainers in forming objectives for lessons that develop learning and understanding. The original model from 1956 splits learning and understanding into six broad categories: knowledge, comprehension, application, analysis, synthesis and evaluation. These objectives range from lower order (knowledge) to higher order (evaluation). Different outcome verbs are associated with each category. It was updated and reordered in 2001, with the following categories: Remember, Understand, Apply, Analyse, Evaluate and Create.

See Appendix 2 for more on Bloom's Taxonomy

Effective sessions build on lower order thinking skills and developing higher order thinking, For example:

- You may begin a session structured around 'lower-order thinking', which would include outcome verbs such as 'describe' or 'discuss'. This level establishes knowledge and comprehension, and will often provide a platform for further learning and development to take place.
- Throughout the session you build up to 'higher-order thinking' verbs, such as 'analyse', 'justify' or 'create'. These higher order thinking skills build on the lower level skills, to establish a much deeper understanding.

Moving up a stage requires a learner to build upon previous knowledge and understanding. It takes careful planning by the teacher to ensure that a learner can move from one stage to the next, with activities or tasks to support learning, and with some way to check learning before moving on.

By using Bloom's Taxonomy, you can structure sessions to build on prior knowledge, 'chunking' learning into manageable parts in order to move individuals forward. For more details about the categories and associated verbs see Appendix 2.

Working in different size groups

Using activities with different group sizes, from small groups to pairs to individuals, offers opportunities for learners to work together and get to know each other. As well as helping with motivation, this also provides them with opportunities to build wider skills such as:

- teamwork
- interpersonal skills
- problem-solving
- and a range of other wider skills that will be useful in the workplace.

Creativity and critical thinking

Activities which encourage creativity provide learners with an opportunity to create something new.

Activities which promote critical thinking, will provide opportunities and structure for them to critically question the norms of a subject and find solutions to issues within the topic.

Both of these approaches can really help engage and motivate learners. See page 80 onwards for some possible ideas for activities.

Student involvement in target setting

Goal or target setting provides learners with direction within each area of their learning. It is often supported through one-to-one tutorials, where there is time to discuss progress and offer advice for moving forward with learning.

The timescale needs to allow for the target to be achieved but short enough to be motivational.

Student ownership of the goal-setting process is integral to the completion of the goal. Coaching conversations during a tutorial can often support the process.

Feedback obtained from formative assessment activities can provide students and teachers with information on progress and understanding in order to set appropriate targets.

> **Key tip**
>
> If you find the group are quiet and struggle to contribute, when setting a task ask them to think it through on their own first for a couple of minutes, then work in pairs, and finally share ideas in a small group, culminating in a group discussion. This builds confidence.

> Targets set should follow the **SMART** acronym:
>
> S – Specific
>
> M – Measurable:
>
> A – Achievable:
>
> R – Relevant: Is
>
> T – Timescale:

Case Study

Tosin writes down the following target: "I want to complete my course soon."

1. Why does this not follow the SMART acronym (see page 36).
2. How could this target be improved?

Tosin writes this target down:

"I will complete my BTEC Extended Diploma to D*D*D* level by June by making clear notes on the distinction tasks for assignments in Unit 1, 2, and 3 for semester one, checking I am achieving these criteria by January."

3. Identify each of the SMART acronyms in this statement.

LO2

Providing feedback

Positive feedback and praise can support learners in building confidence and feeling motivated to develop their learning. Equally, developmental feedback, delivered at the right time and understood by the learner, can offer clear information about what still needs to be worked on.

Offering learners opportunities to quickly act on feedback will reinforce the correction and development of their learning.

> For example, a short exam question is worked through as a group with actions and feedback identified. Learners could then be offered a similar style question to complete as an individual.

See page 95 for more on feedback

Planning and structuring feedback within a session will support the motivation and engagement of individual students.

From an organisational perspective, Ofsted currently look for signs that:

- learners know what progress they are making
- there are regular opportunities for clear feedback to learners
- progress is reviewed within sessions.

2.4 Summarise ways to establish ground rules with learners

As discussed in Chapter 1, the importance of setting ground rules within a group and session provides the basis for the management of the classroom. This in turn provides a safe, supportive, and inclusive space for learners.

How best to establish the ground rules then depends on a number of factors:

- What age and maturity are the group?
- How much guidance will they need to create reasonable ground rules?
- How much time do you have with the group?
- Is it a one-off short session or the start of a lengthy course? This will determine how much time you want to spend on the activity of agreeing the ground rules.

Whatever your answers are to these questions, to create usable ground rules there needs to be student participation and ownership.

Establishing ground rules – possible methods

- A paired or small group discussion to create the list for a whole class agreement.
- Using post-its or whiteboard pens, everyone writes ground rule ideas on the board, and groups them into themes to find agreement.

- A pre-written list of rules is discussed and debated in order to tease out agreement.

All methods require the careful management of negotiations to come to a consensus and create buy-in from learners. There needs to be space to encourage and value all contributions, and celebrate diversity of opinion within a group, whilst maintaining some 'red lines'.

A teacher will also need to ensure their own personal and professional boundaries are upheld within the ground rules. A common example of this is around appropriateness of swearing within the classroom. In some industries and workplaces swearing goes unnoticed and is almost expected – however, the questions for the teacher are:

- What is appropriate within their learning space?
- Would swearing within the classroom create a less or more inclusive environment?

Establishing ground rules provides a strong foundation for a respectful classroom and how it will be managed moving forward. Establishing ground rules in this way also links to the motivational tools discussed earlier, where individual learners feel heard, understood, and like they belong in the learning space. Once established, these rules provide the background to creating an inclusive learning environment.

See Unit 1 LO1 for more on managing behaviour

Activity

Refer back to Chapter 1 and Learning Outcome 2.2 'Why it is important to promote appropriate behaviour and respect for others'. Consider how you use ground rules to create a safe and inclusive classroom.

Reflection

How do you motivate learners in sessions? What could you develop to enable all learners to be motivated and engaged in your sessions?

Key tips for writing AET assignments

As part of your AET assessment writing consider the following points:

- Provide details of the benefits of creating an inclusive learning environment – and also what would happen if you didn't create one.
- Include information that demonstrates how you will create an inclusive learning environment and use information about your learners to promote inclusion.
- Examine your strategies and understanding of how to motivate learners, providing real examples where you can.
- Be clear about ground rules with how and why you would establish them.

LO3 Be able to plan inclusive teaching and learning

> 3.1 Devise an inclusive teaching and learning plan.
>
> 3.2 Justify own selection of teaching and learning approaches, resources and assessment methods in relation to meeting individual learner needs.

As you begin the process of planning your microteach lesson, consideration should be given to the topic of your lesson. Choose something you are knowledgeable and interested in, such as a hobby, interest, or something you might want to teach in the future. Being able to answer wider questions about your subject will enhance your delivery of the session, so choosing a topic you are confident talking about will really help.

Some memorable microteach topics that we have seen include:

- mixing your own spices
- creating and using Play-Doh for fine motor skills
- doing a card trick
- changing a car tyre
- creating choux pastry
- stretches for shoulder mobility
- boxing for exercise.

Remember to establish the prior knowledge that your microteach audience may have of your subject. Plan your session to meet their knowledge and experience of your subject. This could be done through a show of hands or a quick questioning activity to establish where they are as a group with your topic.

Easy questions that can establish this initial assessment include:

- 'What do you know about …?'
- 'Who has experience of …?'

3.1 Devise an inclusive teaching and learning plan

There are many different versions of a lesson plan. Within your AET course, your teacher will offer you a lesson plan template. The lesson plan is an important part of the microteach assessment.

A lesson plan is also an important part of planning and preparation for any session. It can also be used by someone else to deliver the session if you are unable to. Fundamentally, it is your guide to ensuring you have considered all the components for an engaging and inclusive session.

At the planning stage, the learning plan will offer prompts to ensure you have thought about individuals within your session with additional needs. The plan will also highlight your choices of learning activities and you will be able to see how much passive and active learning is taking place. Additionally, the plan will include reminders of any resources you need printed out or to be available in the room e.g. handouts, flipchart paper and pens, an online quiz etc.

Questions to consider when planning your microteach:

- How will you make the session stimulating? What is the 'hook' that will engage learners with the topic? Can you create a relevant story to help learners see the purpose or point of the learning?

- What will move the learning from a passive mode to an active mode, where new knowledge is moved from the working memory to long-term memory for retrieval in the future?

- How will you engage with your learners, to get to know them and be able to motivate them within the session?

- How will you create a balanced lesson, including a variety of teaching and learning methods and approaches?

On the next page is an example of a simple lesson plan layout.

Including timing for the session activities ensures you meet the planned outcomes of the session.

Features of a lesson plan

Aims and Objectives

The aim might be an overarching element of a qualification syllabus or a principle that learners need to know and understand. For example, an aim might be: **Understand the different methods of learning activities and how to choose them**.

The objectives or outcomes of the session are the main pillars of the session structure. They are like the 'to do' list. They should start with a verb (a doing word) such as 'describe' or 'list'. It is useful to have Bloom's Taxonomy on hand when setting objectives. However, a word of caution: NEVER use the word 'understand' to start an objective. Why? Because we want to use verbs that can be measured against the learning.

> **aim** what we are trying to achieve overall – the big picture
>
> **objective** the steps we need to take to meet the aim

LO3

Session Plan Proforma					
Learning Group		Session Number		Date	
Location		Trainer/Teacher/Tutor			

Resources necessary for session	Needs for Differentiation
<ul><li></li><li></li><li></li></ul>	
Aim of the session:	At the end of this session, learners will be able to (Objectives):<ul><li></li><li></li><li></li></ul>

Key skills/functional skills/embedding minimum core	

Timing	Topic/Content knowledge/skills	Teacher Activity	Learning Activities	Learning Checks

Self-Evaluation

Issues Arising:
- Little context with the monologue at the beginning of the class – needs more setting up.
- Consider an alternative idea for if students do not want to get up and perform.

Strengths:
- Clear set out objectives for the session.
- Good participation piece.
- Key words on the whiteboard.
- The passion behind the subject.

Possible changes/alternative approaches/ICT opportunities:
- Video example comes in too early in the session and the video was too long.
- More discussion added into the session

Reproduced with permission from Shrewsbury Colleges Group

For example, 'list five teaching methods', means you can check this has been achieved by seeing the list. However, an objective that states 'understand five teaching methods' is not measurable. The word 'understand' can be used within an aim, but never as an objective.

Examples of possible objectives are as follows. Note that using the sentence 'By the end of this session learners will be able to...' allows the objective to become a phrase that indicates what will be learnt and how it will be learnt. This approach forces you to consider exactly what the learners should come away from the session with.

By the end of the session learners will be able to:

- *Describe a selection of active and passive learning methods.*
- *Explain the strengths and limitations of a selection of learning methods.*
- *Create the aims and objectives for their microteach.*

The verbs at the beginning of each objective then lead the teacher to determine how best to assess that the learning has been achieved:

- *Describe* – could be assessed by an observed discussion of the whole class or in groups
- *Explain* – could be learner responses on a gapped handout or question paper
- *Create* – could be the completion of the start of the microteach pro-forma

In this way we have created a solid basis for a progressive, engaging and inclusive session which has direction and achievements along the way. It is good practice to share these objectives with the group at the beginning of the session. It could be likened to an agenda in a meeting, so that everyone understands where we are going and what we have achieved so far.

Starter activities

Starter activities are a good way to prepare learners for the session ahead. They can help focus the mind and bring attention to the subject. These activities can also be used to recall prior knowledge and understanding of a subject before launching into new learning. Examples of starters include:

- simple games
- quizzes or recap tests
- quick-fire questioning.

Good starter activities ease learners into the lesson because they already know something about the topic. A starter activity can also highlight gaps in knowledge and offers the teacher or trainer an opportunity to support small groups or individuals with interventions to improve understanding.

This approach also allows any learners who missed a session to have a glimpse of what they missed and understand where it fits into the big picture.

Sometimes the 'starter-recap' will highlight glaring knowledge gaps across the whole class. Where a whole-class gap appears it is worth reflecting on the previous session, to see what could be done better next time.

Here are some starter activity ideas:

Name	Equipment	Instructions
Recap Relay	Flipchart or A3 paper and Blu-Tack Coloured marker pens Wall space	• Class is split into teams. • Each team stands in a line next to their own flipchart on the wall. Their coloured pen is the baton for the relay. • Each member of the team goes to the paper and adds a point they remember from the topic. You can make this part as specific or loose as you need. • The team can support each other once it gets hard to remember. • Give clear guidance on what the points system is based on and the time constraint. • Ensure there are no trip hazards. On your marks, get set, go...
Quick Quiz	Prior creation of a short quiz on a web-based package such as: Quizlet, MS Forms, Kahoot, Nearpod, Mentimeter etc. Learners will need access to computer screen/smartphone etc.	• Set up questions to link recall of prior information to what is coming in the session. • Multiple choice questions work well to support the selection of the right answer. • It is best if you can view learner responses so you can provide necessary support to each individual through the session.

Icebreakers

Icebreakers tend to be used at the beginning of a programme of study, or when a new group comes together. They support learners to get to know the topic as well as each other.

Energisers

Energisers are very similar in concept to Starters, except they are used during a session. Energisers can be fun activities which are used to offer a change of pace or energy midway through a session. They are needed when something difficult has led to deep concentration followed by a drop in energy.

Teacher activities / Learning activities

The plan should include prompts for what teacher and learner activities will take place. Once the plan is complete, you should look carefully at these two sections again to make sure there is a good balance between the teacher voice and the active learner participation.

- If the teacher is planning to talk for too long then there will be too much passive learning, which will reduce engagement and is less likely to lead to deeper understanding.
- If the students are constantly active with no instruction or context they will not fully understand the learning objectives nor feel that they are making progress.

Here are some learning activity ideas:

Name	Equipment	Instructions
Class quiz	Paper and pens	• Each learner comes up with two questions – one main question and one back-up if their main question is taken by others in the group. • Questions are based on the topic we are looking to recall. • The key instruction is that they must know the correct answer to their question. • Each learner writes the number of learners/questions on their quiz paper, and then each learner in turn asks their own question. • Everyone writes down their answers. Keep a note of the order, ready for the answers round. • After all the questions have been asked, the answer round is used to highlight who feels confident to answer the questions, with the students confirming whether the answers are accurate. • Answers can be self-marked or swapped • Scores can be recorded, or use a show of hands e.g. 'who scored over 10?'. • This can be managed as a team quiz if you have a large group – this can save time and the mixing of learners within groups can support learners who have missed sessions etc.

LO3

Round Robin	Several sheets of A3 paper, each laid down on a different table in the room Each sheet of paper has a different topic heading in the middle, in a mind map style.	• Write the topic headings on the sheets. • Split the class into smaller groups and assign each to one table. • Within a time limit they should write all they can remember about that heading, clearly and neatly on the sheet. • When time is up the groups move to the next table to add to the next heading, • Time should be split between the reading the previous group's answers and adding their own. • This activity continues until all groups have visited all tables • The groups could be asked to create a presentation about the class's ideas from the sheet they land on. At the end of each presentation the class are tasked to either add one more thing to the heading or ask a question of the presenting group, to further expand one of their points.
Exam question	Have an exam or test question ready on the board or in paper form.	• Learners can quietly process their knowledge and understanding of a topic by answering a question or a series of questions on the prior knowledge. • Demonstrating a model answer can support learners to remember further key points. • Use of a visualiser (which is a copy of a good answer up on the big screen) can help here – learners can then see where they have completed something well, or where they need to develop their answers. • This approach is helpful not just for courses with exams but where prior knowledge will be assessed and needs to be understand before moving onto the next topic.
Pub Quiz	Paper and pens	• Learners are split into teams and each team designs questions about the topic covered so far. • Teams need to write a list of 5-10 questions – the number of questions depends on number of teams and time. • Each team takes it in turn to be quiz master, asking their questions and giving the correct answer.

Team-building activities

Place the stick on the ground

- This is a good team-building activity:
- Place learners in teams of 3-4.
- Each team has is given a long cane or stick.
- As a group they stand in a line with their index fingers pointing out.
- The stick is laid along all their fingers.
- The goal is, as a group, to place the stick lengthways, on the floor, without it dropping or one part landing before the other.

Build a bridge

This is a good team problem-solving activity. Learners are placed in small groups and asked to build a bridge between two desks or other surfaces. They can be given specific materials to use, such as recycled paper or paper towels. The idea is that the group pools ideas and solutions to build a bridge that can hold the heaviest weight.

There are many other problem-solving group activities, such as the Tower of Hanoi. You can search the internet for variations on this and many other problems. Some are physical puzzles and some are online, so you can use whatever is most suitable for your session.

Communication activities

Back to back drawings

- Divide the group into pairs. Each person in the pair labels themselves as A or B.
- They sit back-to-back on chairs, each with a pen, paper and something to lean on.
- The aim is for A to be able to explain to B their drawing in such a way that B can draw it accurately.
- A goes first and draws a simple picture e.g. a house, tree, boat, or famous landmark
- The teacher/trainer calls time, and A then needs to describe their picture to B without stating what it is (i.e. saying 'it's a boat').
- Learner B attempts to draw A's picture.
- After a set amount of time A and B can compare their two pictures.
- Each pair can display their two pictures to the rest of the class. A class discussion about which pairs were better able to recreate pictures, and why that might be, leads to a discussion about communication skills.
- This activity can be adapted for different ages and levels by using further rules about what can or can't be described, such as 'no shape words to be used'. Or the drawing can be more challenging e.g. 'create a map and describe the directions to a place'.

Physical games

Group juggle

- You will need a number of tennis or juggling balls, or mini bean bags.
- Stand the group in a circle.
- The aim is to get one ball to every person in the group. The ball should not go in order around the circle, but instead thrown randomly from one person to the next, using their name.
- The group has to remember the order the ball went in.
- Once the order is established the goal is to get one ball through the same sequence in the fastest time.
- Pausing to ask how this could be made faster/easier will evoke a conversation around the team working together.
- Once the group is confident with one ball a second is added, slowly at first but then at increasing speed.
- More balls are added to the group juggle.
- If a ball is dropped the sequence is started again. You can pause to discuss how to prevent dropping the ball i.e. ensuring the catcher is ready and has their eye on the thrower before the ball is thrown.
- The juggle ends on the best/fastest sequence of multiple ball juggles.

There is a metaphor attached to this game. In studies and in life it can feel like a group juggle – there are many elements to what is happening and things can often feel very chaotic and fast. However if we focus on the elements we can control, in this case how we catch and throw one ball, we can meet the challenge. We have to accept that we will sometimes drop a ball. This can happen – we just need to acknowledge that we have a lot going on, but will look at what could be done better next time, with the support of our team.

Online quizzes and games

Quizzes can be used in main class activities as well as in Starters. Common quiz providers include Kahoot, Quizlet and Puzzlemaker. These are useful to repeat over time and offer a quick check of learning.

Plenary activities

A **plenary** is an activity that is often used at the end of a session to check that learning has taken place. They are used by teachers and trainers during or at the end of the session to review and consolidate learning.

On the next page are some quick wins – examples of plenary ideas that can be used for assessment.

Scaling for confidence in a subject	On a scale of 1-10, How confident are you in this topic? What would take you 1 or 2 points higher?
Questioning techniques (Many options for this - search TES online for further ideas)	Open questions – What, When, Why, How?
	Closed questions – Agree or disagree statements.
	Yes or no answers.
	Direct (named) questioning.
	Whole-class questioning using mini whiteboards or online tools and quizzes.
Student-led presentation of research	Following a researched presentation by students, the audience pose questions to check and understand knowledge.
Pub Quiz approach - or using the format of game shows	Scoring points and possibly winning prizes. Could be in pairs, teams, or individuals. Fun and fast.

Assessment activities

You can use all of the activities we have discussed for formative assessment. 'Formative assessment', 'learning or progress checks', and 'Assessment for Learning' activities are different names for checking that the learning we set out to do has been achieved. Choosing appropriate assessment activities within the lesson plan guides the session towards meeting its objectives.

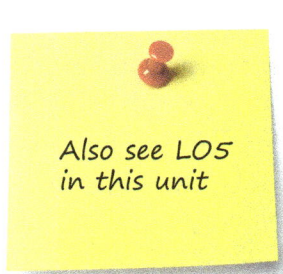

Also see LO5 in this unit

For example a small group discussion, with students presenting back key points, would assess the progress of learners whilst they are gathering knowledge from each other.

Some assessment methods may:

- be observed – such as a practical demonstration
- be written – such as a quiz or written question
- come from questioning individuals and the group.

There are many forms of assessment that can be used within any session and the next chapter will cover these in greater detail.

Resources

It helps to be clear in advance about what you will need to deliver the session, so that part of your preparation includes sourcing these resources. This could include:

- getting copies of activities ready
- setting up practical activities
- a prompt to have IT available
- finding coloured paper and pens.

Whatever you need to deliver the lesson should be listed in the plan so you can check them off and be prepared.

Timing

Another key aspect of the plan is how long each element of the session will take. When you have a short session, such as the microteach, it is particularly important to be realistic about the timings for each activity, to ensure you complete everything you plan for.

It is often at this planning stage that student-teachers realise their microteach topic will need to be cut down to something smaller and more specific. Keeping spoken delivery short and specific will leave more time available to the learning activities. It is important to remember that the microteach is a lesson and not a presentation.

Practice delivering your microteach session to an audience, in order to see where timings need to be adapted before the actual assessment.

Mixing up sessions

It is normally worth having a few, ice-breaker or energiser activities available, in order to change the energy of the session. This is often useful after a detailed or thought-provoking section, to allow the brain to focus on something else for a while.

Evaluation

Most lesson plan formats will have a section for evaluating the session. This gives you space to jot some simple notes to indicate where the lesson worked and where you might make changes for the next time you deliver the session.

It is worth noting your initial thoughts on the session immediately, as memory can distort what actually happened if left for too long. We will explore evaluation in detail in LO5 of this chapter.

Teaching takeaways

Once you have completed your plan, in principle it is worth creating presentation slides to give structure to your lesson. Many established teachers and trainers do not need a presentation to structure their lessons; however it is a useful tool to ensure you stay on track and offer prompts for the next activity or instructions to learners.

Remember to establish prior knowledge of your microteach subject with the peers that you will be delivering your microteach to. Plan how you might use the 'expert in the room', if there is someone who has knowledge of your subject.

Activity

Create a toolkit of different activities that you can refer to when planning different sessions.

Ideas for teaching...

Have a bank of starters, icebreakers and energisers, plenary activities, recap games, and retrieval approaches to use within your sessions. Humans like routine, it helps us feel safe and secure. One idea is to ensure your lesson plan has a similar structure each time e.g.:

Starter: as they arrive into the room – this could be an activity on desks, on the whiteboard or on the screen e.g a question.

Recap: once everyone is settled and the session is introduced, this is used as a way to remind them what they learnt last session and to understand what prior learning they have on a subject before launching into new content.

Retrieval: retrieval activities embed past learning by linking it to new learning. Spaced retrieval helps new learning to become part of the long term memory and enables information to be retrieved readily.

Content of new learning: consider the cone of experience (page 61) to vary how this is delivered. Consider the size of 'chunks' of new information – how much is enough and how will you check they have understood it?

Energiser: used to switch the brain on again; these are quick and can even involve moving their bodies.

Plenary: used to check understanding of the session content. Review as many assessment for learning strategies as you can to have options and alternatives. This section of a lesson helps to consolidate learning.

Reflection

What will be the main considerations for creating an inclusive lesson for your microteach? How will you use this understanding for your future lessons?

Case Study

It is important to reflect on success, and areas to develop, after delivering a session.

Rolfe's reflective practice model is a simple and quick approach to use. There are further prompting questions available on the internet, or you can just use the prompts here to reflect on your teaching or training sessions.

Using Rolfe's method, examine and reflect on a session you have delivered. Consider:

- what worked well,
- what didn't go so well
- what you would do differently next time.

Use this to help you plan for the next session.

Rolfe's model of reflection (2001)

LO3

3.2 Justify own selection of teaching and learning approaches, resources and assessment methods in relation to meeting individual learner needs

You will be asked to provide a rationale and justify your choice of activities and approaches within your microteach. This indicates to your assessor that you understand the individual needs of your particular group of learners, and that you have considered how to address them with your chosen methods. This aspect of the assessment is often assessed through a one-to-one tutorial with your AET teacher, alongside the actual delivery of the microteach.

At the planning stage of the microteach it is important to demonstrate an understanding of the varied approaches that could have been chosen to support the session aims and objectives. The plan should include a mixture of:

- individual activities
- paired work
- small group work
- large group methods.

A balance of learning approaches which are centred around the learner experience, including active learning and experiential learning, all bring inclusivity to the session.

You need to demonstrate that you have considered the sequence of learning:

- Is each new piece of information attached to prior learning and does it build on it to create the full session?
- Are you employing retrieval techniques to reinforce learning and move it from the working memory to long-term memory?

You will also need to show that you are clear about the resources you need and how they will support the learners in the session. Include considerations for:

- adapting resources for specific learning needs
- creating resources which are designed for the level of learning and are stimulating.

Within your justification for your lesson plan you should also reflect on your use and choice of assessment methods throughout the session. Showing that you have given sufficient thought to linking the assessment method to the lesson objective, goes some way to showing that your session is designed to create progress for your learners, and offer opportunities to correct any misconceptions.

Ideas for teaching...

Here's one way you could lay out your justifications for your chosen assessments:

- Create a table and list each of the learners you will be delivering the microteach to.

- Check their understanding or experience of your microteach topic. Include this in your table. Categories could be 'expert', 'some experience', 'no prior knowledge'.

- Check their identified learning needs – how do they describe their learning needs? Add this to your table. Be mindful that this information is sensitive and personal and should be kept secure and private.

- Summarise the group's learning needs

- Think of the different teaching and learning approaches that meet all of these needs, and the different prior knowledge that the learners have.

Ensure you have worked these approaches into your lesson plan.

Activity

Create a list of five ways in which your lesson plan meets the needs of the learners and leads to an inclusive learning environment. You can use this as part of your assessment to justify your planning decisions.

Reflection

Use Rolfe's reflective practice model to consider the planning of your microteach lesson plan. What would you do to improve your planning process?

LO4 Be able to deliver inclusive teaching and learning

4.1 Use teaching and learning approaches, resources and assessment methods to meet individual learner needs.

4.2 Communicate with learners in ways that meet their individual needs.

4.3 Provide constructive feedback to learners to meet their individual needs.

4.1 Use teaching and learning approaches, resources and assessment methods to meet individual learner needs

Lesson organisation

- Make use of your lesson plan before the lesson by having your list of resources ready and in the right order for the session.
- Check your IT is working and ready to go, and be prepared before your learners arrive.
- Be confident with your activities – practice them on a friendly audience before the session.
- Have your lesson plan in clear view to ensure you stay on track and on time.

Pacing

The pace of a lesson is important to move learners on and motivate them to stay engaged with the content:

- too fast and learners may miss the points
- too slow and they may get bored and switch off.

This is where the variety of your chosen activities will help to keep moving the session on, whilst meeting different learners' preferred styles and needs.

Your ability to transition from one activity to the next, with clear instructions of what your learners should do, is a skill worth practicing. Even the best learning activities can lose their impact if the learners do not understand the instructions for what they are supposed to do.

It is important to check understanding of instructions and progress of learning when delivering your session.

- The use of quick assessment methods such as questioning techniques will highlight how learners are progressing.

- Formative assessment methods will check how learners are progressing and also allow you to correct any misconceptions so far.

The assessment guidelines stipulate that you deliver your microteach for a minimum of 15 minutes (we allow 20 minutes for ours) and that you are part of the microteach session for at least an hour, where you will give feedback on each microteach observed.

Monitoring the time and ensuring you know where you are within your session plan is key to delivering successful microteach sessions.

- Being a little nervous, some student-teachers often find that they have raced through their session and need extra activities at the end to meet the timeframe.
- Others often plan to complete too much in their session, or are so invested in their topic that they spend too long on the introduction to complete all the activities, and run out of time.

Assessors will normally give students a warning with five minutes to go and can be a little flexible with the cut-off, in order to give students a fair chance to wrap up their session. However, the timeframe is there for a reason and the assessor is looking for you to be able to manage your time – just as in any real teaching and learning session. The session is purposely tight on time and reflects what will happen at a job interview for a teaching role. Learning to keep track of time whilst providing an interesting, inclusive session is a vital skill for this qualification and any future job role.

You can overcome timing issues by practicing the session to an audience before the real thing, maybe even more than once, keeping a close eye on timings. You can then make adjustments before you perform the real microteach.

Your presence in the classroom should provide an air of confidence, knowledge, and organisation for the learners, which in turn allows them to be relaxed and ready to learn. Some people have had experiences in their lives which gives them this presence. For others it comes with time and practice. Taking feedback, practice, and working on your organisation, will all help to develop a confident approach to the session and cannot be underestimated.

> **Key tip**
> It is important to know how much prior learning there is in your microteach session. If you are providing learning about your hobby or interest, you will probably know a lot more about it than the majority of the AET group. On the other hand there is the possibility that someone in the session could be an expert in the field.

Teaching takeaways

- Take your full lesson plan and reduce it to a shorthand version for timing purposes, so that in the microteach you can keep a quick eye on your timings.
- Practice your session out loud and with an audience, so you can check your explanation of activities make sense.
- Remember your microteach is not a presentation – however much you want to tell the audience about your knowledge, the point is to teach not tell.

LO4

> **Key tip**
>
> Some common pitfalls to try to avoid when delivering the microteach are usually easily remedied if considered beforehand.
>
> - **Running out of material.** Delivering the microteach too quickly, usually because of nerves, can be balanced, by adding an extra activity at the end to utilise the time left.
>
> - **Dealing with nerves.** Nerves are easier to deal with when learners are engaged in the session and the focus is on the learning, as opposed to the presenter. So, set a quick activity as soon as possible. Consider what it is that will show you are nervous and counteract it. For example, have water on hand for a dry mouth and don't hold papers if shaking is a problem. Maintain eye contact with all of the group, don't just focus on one person.
>
> - **Too much content.** If you are going to run out of time, stop, pause, ask learners what they have learned so far, and then summarise and close.
>
> - Make sure you have an **extra copy of your lesson plan** to pass to the assessor.

> **Activity**
>
> Go over your lesson plan for the microteach and create a list of resources you will need for the session.
>
> Begin collecting these in the days running up to the session. Organising your resources in good time will build your confidence. Rushing around in the hours or minutes before the session causes distraction and could reduce confidence.

> **Reflection**
>
> How will you prepare for the delivery of your microteach?

4.2 Communicate with learners in ways that meet their individual needs

Language and pitch

Consideration for the language and pitch of your lessons is vital for the progress and understanding of your learners. Once you have decided on the topic of your microteach, and as you move into developing your sessions, it is important to break the content down to suit the level of the learners. This includes considering what prior knowledge individual learners may have on the subject.

One real-life example which demonstrates this was a microteach where the student-teacher wanted learners to deliver an element of a Shakespeare monologue. The teacher launched straight into the monologue and wanted the group to practice their delivery of it. However, the teacher hadn't checked prior learning, to see if anyone had any understanding of Shakespeare. Nor had they explained what had happened in the play prior to the monologue. There was an international student in the group who had never come across Shakespeare, and others who had not studied his work. The student-teacher recognised the confusion on everyone's faces and was able to rewind and set up some additional building blocks to the activity. However, valuable time was lost in the session, which could have been avoided by considering:

- the level of understanding or familiarity of the learners
- how to break down a subject into the right size and level of sub-sections, sometimes referred to as 'chunks' of learning.

It is clear that verbal communication skills, including listening skills, are important in the role of teacher or trainer. You can improve verbal communication skills by:

- seeking external feedback
- being constructively critical of your own approach
- attempting to assess how well you deliver information and instructions through honest observations of people's reactions.

You can make steps to improve the verbal delivery of a session through:

- not speaking too fast
- the use of pauses
- talking with enthusiasm
- varying your tone
- truly hearing and listening to learners and responding appropriately.

Body language

Our body language and gestures provide many communication cues to an audience of learners. If you watch primary school teachers, they use a huge array of visual cues, so that younger learners receive clear prompts for what to do. We need to be aware that:

- our body language and gestures can both engage and disengage our learners
- we all have body language idiosyncrasies that we may not even be aware of
- these idiosyncrasies may be communicating things to our audience that we are completely unaware of.

Understanding our body language tendencies can further support the communication process within a session.

> **Key tip**
>
> Knowing your own communication strengths and weaknesses is key to developing a strong teaching presence. Seeking feedback on your communication skills, from learners, colleagues and mentors, will support your development. We can't always see issues with our own communication skills, it takes outside constructive feedback to help us improve.

LO4

Enhancing communication

Communication can be enhanced through varied questioning techniques which support all learners and indicate to the teacher who is progressing well and who may need support.

Non-direct questioning allows a less confident learner to respond to a question but still provides information to the teacher about their progress.

More direct questioning on knowledge and understanding can provide a more competitive element and an opportunity for learners to 'show off' progress.

Here are some examples of question types.

Non-direct questioning	More direct questioning
Whiteboards to provide answers on – all show their answers at the same time	Hands up.
Multichoice questions – using cards to show response – coloured cards or lettered cards	Named person answers.
Post-it notes on a board	Pose, pause, ask, bounce: Pose the question, leave a pause, ask an individual, bounce the right or wrong answer to another individual for clarification or additional information.
Written quizzes – taken in and marked by the teacher	Quizzes marked by other students.
Online quizzes – answers seen by individual student and teacher only	Round the room, everyone answers. Chair Bingo – everyone stands up and to sit down again they must answer a question on the topic so far.

> **Reflection**
>
> How do you know your strengths in communication skills? Where are your blind spots i.e. What don't you know and how will you improve in this area of communication?

Activity

Video record yourself practicing your microteach or other delivered session and watch it back. Be aware of your body language, the clarity of your explanations and the way you speak. Whilst this footage can be difficult to watch, it provides a great opportunity to improve your communication style.

4.3 Provide constructive feedback to learners to meet their individual needs

Feedback is a powerful tool in the teaching process and, managed well, it can build confidence and engage learners. Used less effectively, it can have the opposite effect and leave learners confused, disheartened and disengaged with their learning. Different approaches to feedback are a necessary skill for a teacher or trainer to ensure we are meeting the needs of the individual learner.

Within your microteach session much of the feedback you'll provide will be in the form of praise, and this shouldn't be underestimated in terms of the impact it has on the student's sense of confidence. Similarly, when feedback is given by peers at the end of each microteach the emphasis is on what went well in the session, with development points offered in a balanced and positive way.

Within any session, making praise specific to an activity, effort or skill ensures the feedback isn't vague and doesn't sound disingenuous. So rather than:

> *'Well done, everyone.'*

be specific:

> *'Excellent effort on what is a difficult maths task, it was great to see you all helping each other.'*

Posing public questions

You need to consider how you will respond to an incorrect answer to a question you have posed. For some learners it can be crushing to have a public answer highlighted as incorrect – some of them may never try to answer a question again. However, it is important that learners understand where they have gone wrong. Often using a phrase such as:

> *'Close, but not quite right – can anyone else explain?'*

or

> *'I can see why you might think that, but not quite what I'm looking for'*

are softer responses than an outright 'no, that is incorrect'. You can re-phase your question, if you feel that could help the learner answer correctly.

Feedback on work

Where learners receive feedback to improve their work, it is important that:

- the comments are appropriate to their level of learning
- the comments are specific to the work they are demonstrating
- the feedback is understood and can be actioned quickly to show improvement.

In your microteach session you can demonstrate this approach by asking learners to complete a task again using feedback which enables them to demonstrate progress.

When planning your microteach session, consider whether peer-assessment or self-assessment methods could provide feedback to the learners. When deciding on peer and self-assessment activities you should prepare clear guidance for what the assessment will focus on. These assessments take careful management, because you want to ensure learners do feel the benefit of praise from you, the teacher. Both can be effective ways to build a supportive approach to improving a skill, because in self-assessment learners are marking their own work and can see clearly their mistakes without anyone else highlighting them. In peer assessment they have a trusted peer to assess them, but also get to view someone else's approach to the work.

peer-assessment – when learners assess one another's work in line with a set of assessment criteria.

self-assessment – when the individual assesses their own work and applies certain assessment criteria.

During the microteach assessment, as well as delivering your own session you will be expected to give feedback to your peers on their lessons. A popular approach to delivering verbal feedback in public is to use the 'feedback sandwich'. This consists of:

- specific praise on an element of the session
- specific development or improvement point
- finish with another praise point.

You may also be asked to provide written feedback that the student teacher can take away and reflect on. A feedback form may look something like the example on the next page.

Again, it is important that the student teacher understands how they can improve their lessons as well as knowing what they did well.

Feedback that helps a learner develop is sometimes known as **feedforward** as it helps them move their learning and practice forwards.

Key tip
- Prepare positive feedback responses to an incorrect answer
- Consider an 80 to 20 ratio for Praise to Correction
- Plan for self-assessment and peer assessment activities

Session date:	Delivered by:
Title of session:	Length of session:

Good Practice identified:

Areas for development:

What have I learnt that can influence my own practice:

This feedback can remain confidential, or you may sign your name if you wish.

Name: _____ Date: _____

Signature:

Teaching takeaways

When giving feedback it is often helpful to check what the learner understood from your comments. This allows you to assess their perception of your words, and enables you to manage any further confusion in the activity or task.

Activity

Be aware within your AET session or when observing a teacher how often they provide feedback to learners through praise or correction. Make a note of what works for you and what approaches you will build into your practice.

Reflection

How do you feel after feedback? What feedback approaches helped to develop your skills and understanding? Why did this approach work for you?

LO5 Be able to evaluate the delivery of inclusive teaching and learning

5.1 Review the effectiveness of own delivery of inclusive teaching and learning.

5.2 Identify areas for improvement in own delivery of inclusive teaching and learning.

5.1 Review the effectiveness of own delivery of inclusive teaching and learning

5.2 Identify areas for improvement in own delivery of inclusive teaching and learning

It is important to be able to examine what you did well in addition to how you will improve. Often learners go straight into what they would do differently, or what didn't work, without giving themselves credit and reflecting on what did go well. Treat yourself as you would do a learner and give specific self-praise where it is due.

Following on from your microteach there are a number of sources of feedback which will enable you to review the effectiveness of your lesson:

- Your teacher will have given you written and verbal feedback.
- Your peers will have given you written and verbal feedback.
- You will have your own interpretation of how the lesson went.
- Finally, you may have access to a video recording of your microteach, so you can review it again. (Only the bravest students ever ask to review their recording for self-reflection but it is an incredibly useful activity).

There are also different times for you to reflect on the microteach:

- Immediately after your session jot down a few thoughts on what went well and what you would do differently. Use the section of your lesson plan for these short notes.
- At the end of the session, consider what you learnt about delivering a lesson from your peers.
- When you come to write this part of your assignment, review the feedback and notes again to see if any other thoughts come to you.

When writing up your review consider the different elements of your session. The table of questions on the next page could help consolidate your thoughts.

There are many reflective models that can be used when you consider the effectiveness of your teaching and learning practices.

Brookfield's Reflective Lenses

One model, which combines the elements of feedback that you will have received, is Brookfield's Reflective Lenses, which asks you to consider the feedback received from the observer, the learners, your own reflections and relevant theories.

Using the questions below, reflect on the specific parts of your microteach session; this will support your development plan.

Was the choice of topic and teaching approaches effective?	How effective was the instruction and delivery of the activities?
Was your communication clear and effective?	Did you listen and respond to learners effectively?
How much did your peers engage with the activities you designed?	Were your peers enthusiastic about your session?
Were your peers quick to get going with your lesson activities?	Did they ask further questions and respond to your questions?
How well did you manage to cover all you had planned and how well did you meet your session objectives?	How did your timing of the session and activities go?

Activity

Prior to your microteach or a session you are going to deliver, go though these questions and adapt your plan if necessary.

Ideas for teaching...

Prepare for the review before you deliver your microteach session, so that you have a mechanism to record your thoughts. Emotions are often high after the session is delivered – this a great time to record your reflections on the session 'in the moment'.

Reflection

After the microteach, consider what the teaching experience felt like and concentrate on the positive elements of the session.

Once you have reflected on your session you will begin to understand where you need to make improvements for your teaching development. You can continue this process by thinking about specific aspects of your delivery and considering actions to take.

More specific aspects include:

Aspect of delivery	Considerations
Subject knowledge	What is the latest thinking or research or activity in my subject, am I up to date?
Teaching Approaches	What other activities could I have chosen that would give an improved learning experience?
Planning	Did I feel organised and in control of the session? What else could I do to improve the planning of my sessions?
Timing and pacing	Did some activities take longer than I thought? Remember this for next time. Did some activities or questioning take less time? What else could I include to extend this?
Classroom management	How well did the session flow? Was I able to respond to each learner in a timely way? How could I manage the space better? What else do I need to improve for more challenging learners?
Managing individual and group activities	How well did I provide instructions? How could I do this differently? How well did I manage the transition between activities? Were they in the right order for sequencing learning? How did I use learners prior knowledge to adapt activities?
Learner-centred approaches	Did I (the teacher) do too much of the work? On balance, was my session active and engaging for the learners? Or was it too passive? How can I check this in future sessions?
Communication skills	How clear were my instructions? Did I hear all the learners? Did I respond to their needs verbally? What was my body language like? What could I do to improve?
Feedback	How effective was my feedback to learners? How well did I use praise and positive reinforcement? How effective were my corrections?

Considering these questions should enable you to evaluate areas for improvement and create a clear action plan for improving your practice and developing your skills.

Teaching takeaways

Throughout your teaching and training career you should become used to reflective practice and constant improvement of skills. It is useful to keep a written log to enable you to see where you have made progress.

> **Reflection**
> What three actions will you take from the microteach into your professional practice?

Activity

Create a checklist of strengths in your practice from your own perspective and the feedback from tutors and peers.

Post-it feedback is a good way to help you to develop inclusive sessions. At the end of the session ask for one post-it with what the learners enjoyed about the session, and one element that they would want less of. This way you get to see how to improve the sessions to meet the individual needs of the group. Share the results, so they can see how you have made changes.

Key tips

Assessment top tips for AET assignments:

- Start thinking about your microteach topic early.
- Consider which activities will best 'teach' the topic.
- Practice the microteach with a timer and audience before the assessment.
- Get resources ready early for a calm approach to the microteach.
- Remember to note down, hear and accept the positive feedback as much as learning from the suggestions for improvement.

Reflection

- What new teaching approaches will you try out?
- How will you ensure your lesson planning has a logical sequence and supports all learners?
- What are your considerations for lesson planning?
- How will you assess and improve your communication skills?
- What reflective tools will you use to evaluate your lessons?

Chapter 3 Understanding Assessment in Education and Training

Assessment is often a confusing concept to break down. The simplest way to describe assessment is 'a check that learning has taken place'. This may sound very simple and straightforward. However, the process of checking actual learning against intended learning is far more complex. Assessment, at its finest, helps to inform different areas of teaching and training and acts as a review of the teaching and learning process, as it can inform methods and teaching practices to suit learners. This chapter aims to explain what assessment is, the methods used to effectively assess learning, how we can build on the foundations of learning to incite deeper learning and, finally, how we can record this for all stakeholders involved.

> LO1: Understand types and methods of assessment used in education and training.
>
> LO2: Understand how to involve learners and others in the assessment process.
>
> LO3: Understand the role and use of constructive feedback in the assessment process.
>
> LO4: Understand requirements for keeping records of assessment in education and training.

LO1 Understand types and methods of assessment used in education and training

> 1.1 Explain the purposes of types of assessment used in education and training.
>
> 1.2 Describe characteristics of different methods of assessment in education and training.
>
> 1.3 Compare the strengths and limitations of different assessment methods in relation to meeting individual learner needs.
>
> 1.4 Explain how different assessment methods can be adapted to meet individual learner needs.

1.1 Explain the purposes of types of assessment used in education and training

Assessment means checking that learning has taken place. It might be assumed that assessment is only the final piece of the educational jigsaw, such as the final activity that takes place. However, in actual fact, assessment starts as soon as a learner displays an interest in attending a course.

You are probably more familiar with your understanding of assessment than you realise. Throughout education, you will have been assessed at various points, whether informally (off the record) or formally (for the record).

There are a number of different reasons why assessment is carried out:

- To determine your educational level at a certain stage in your life (e.g. SATs, GCSE etc).
- To determine if you have the knowledge and understanding to progress on to something else or another qualification.
- To demonstrate knowledge and understanding of a particular subject.
- Within job interviews, to try and predict your performance in a job role.

The type of assessment can vary depending on the reason for the assessment.

Let's start by looking at the most commonly known types of assessment:

Initial assessment

This type of assessment takes place at the start of the learning process. Initial assessment aims to determine the starting point for a learner: what knowledge and skills do they arrive with?

Methods of gathering this information can vary:

- It could be an application form, with a request for details of previous education, qualifications, and any declarations of learning needs.
- It could be a pre-course interview, where the learner is asked questions and their knowledge and skills are tested.
- It could also be the first session of the course, where the teacher or trainer observes behaviours, attitudes and skills.

From the initial assessment, as teachers or trainers we can then plan how we teach the course, which teaching strategies will be effective and which less so.

Diagnostic assessment

Identifying gaps in knowledge and skills is key. When teaching a group, learners will all be at different levels and abilities. Diagnostic assessments are used to test current knowledge and understanding and identify any gaps. This informs planning for future sessions, in order to plug the gaps, and helps with setting realistic goals for each individual.

Formative assessment

Formative assessment is ongoing assessment. It is informal, so it's not always recorded, but it is vital and crucial to the learning and teaching process. Students on the AET course sometimes struggle to grasp this type of assessment.

Common examples of formative assessment are questioning and observation, completed by the teacher as the session progresses. This can inform you if a learner (or group) has understood a concept. By asking questions of the group or individuals, you can assess if learning has taken place, and if the message has been understood. It can be as simple as someone's facial expressions indicating that they are struggling to understand; or you can infer something about understanding through the questions the learner is asking you to help clarify points. This kind of formative assessment can really test a teacher's experience and intuition.

Formative assessment is ongoing because it never really stops. As a teacher or trainer, you will be constantly assessing the learners, the group and the impact of the key points you are making. Your experience and intuition will help guide you through this. The more you teach, the more you will tune these skills and be able to read and interpret signs as they present.

Dylan Wiliam, a Welsh educationalist is a big advocate of formative assessment and is described as the 'father of formative assessment'. He is the author of 'Inside the Black Box' and has spent many years researching the impact of formative assessment and promotes the methodology as opposed to summative assessment.

Formative assessment is also known as Assessment for Learning (AfL) because it can help inform teaching strategies and future learning required to move the learner forward.

Wiliam (11 Sept 2018) explains this well in this video on YouTube:

https://tinyurl.com/mpebjh9y

In this video he asks the following questions:

- Where is the learner going?
- Where are they now?
- What do we need to help them get there?

Summative assessment

Summative assessment provides a summary of learning. It is usually a formal method of assessment that is recorded and which provides an outcome. Summative assessment methods include:

- exams
- assignments
- tests.

These are final measures that determine a learner's outcome. Also known as Assessment of Learning (AoL), it is often recorded in the form of a grade or mark. It tests the learner's knowledge and skills at the point of exit. This can be the exit of the course, qualification, or module.

Summative assessment is usually at the end of a subject as it measures the learning that has taken place. Within a formal qualification it is often linked to an assessment grade and governed by standards and criteria set by an awarding body. For example, there are summative assessment standards on the AET, so your teacher will check that the work you have submitted meets these set criteria.

Some courses have a pass, merit, or distinction grading, some just use pass or fail, and others are given a percentage mark or number grade. It is important for learners that they understand the method and criteria they are assessed against, so that they know what the expectations are. We will examine this a little later in the chapter.

Holistic assessment

Holistic assessment is a collection of assessment methods that measure outcomes in many different ways. A great example of this is the AET microteach. Completing the microteach will mean that you will construct a lesson plan, show evidence of considering learner needs, embed the core skills, deliver the session and then evaluate the lesson after. Within this task there are a lot of assessment methods being used.

1.2 Describe characteristics of different methods of assessment in education and training

1.3 Compare the strengths and limitations of different assessment methods in relation to meeting individual learner needs

When assessing any type of learning, it is important that the learner understands what is required of them. There are some key characteristics to consider when launching an assessment.

In section 1.1 we explored some of the types of assessment. You should now have an overview of what type of assessments are needed, why they are needed and when we need to complete them. Now we will start to consider some of the methods of assessment that are commonly used and what the benefits and pitfalls are of each of those methods.

Activity

List methods of assessment that you have experienced, use within your teaching/training or are aware of, for example:

- Exam
- Coursework
- etc.

Take the top five and consider the benefits and pitfalls of this method of assessment:

Method	Benefit	Pitfall
1. Exam	Measures the learning that has taken place. Same test for all.	Stressful. Timed.

Here is a list of most of the commonly used assessments:

• Exam • Essay/Assignment • Question & Answer • Observation	• Quiz • Presentation • Role play • Practical demonstration	• Research exam • Open book exam • Test

It is not exhaustive and you may have some different examples. Whatever the methods of assessment that you choose, it needs to follow some basic principles that ensure the assessment is fair and consistent. The most common principles of assessment are:

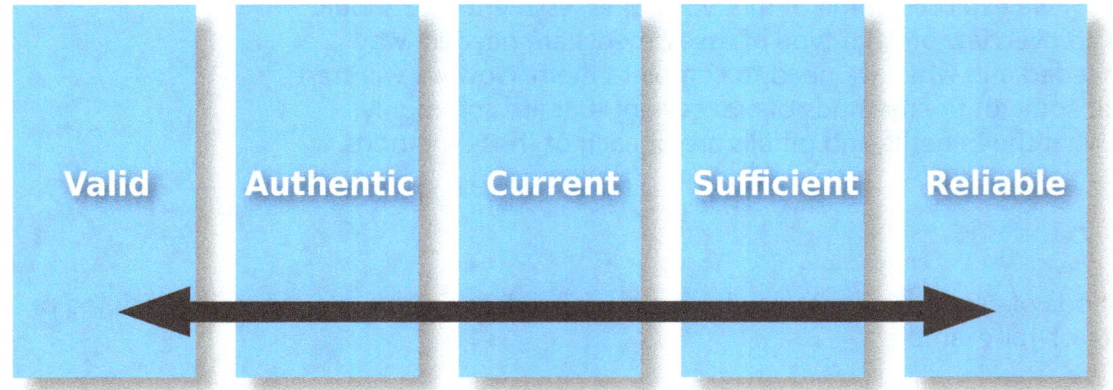

A useful way to describe the five headings above is to consider learning to drive. When learning to drive in the UK you have to pass a theory test and then conduct a practical driving test.

Let's consider the five principles above in the context of learning to drive a vehicle.

Valid

When considering if a method of assessment is valid or not, we need to ask whether the method selected is an appropriate way to test for knowledge and skills.

Is a theory exam appropriate for learning to drive? Yes it is, as long as it is part of the overall assessment method. However it wouldn't be appropriate if there was only a theory exam, because it does not assess the application of knowledge or the skill in operating a car safely on the roads.

Authentic

Authenticity is the check that the right person is completing the assessment.

With the theory test and driving test, a provisional driving licence has to be shown on both occasions so that the examiners can check on the identity of the individual.

Current

Currency is the check that an assessment is up to date and assesses the right skills and knowledge.

The theory test and driving test are kept up to date and current, so they test skills and knowledge that are needed now. Both elements have changed over the years in order to keep relevant.

Sufficient

Does an assessment provide enough information to make an informed decision as to whether that individual is competent or not? If it does, then the assessment is sufficient.

The theory test asks a range of specific questions about a number of different things that a driver is likely to encounter. The number and type of questions are sufficient to ensure that only someone who knows a lot about a range of things can pass.

The driving test is usually along a planned route that checks a wide range of skills (e.g. turning right into main roads, navigating traffic lights, manoeuvres, hill starts, emergency stops etc.) over a set period of time. It is designed so that someone can show the examiner they can handle all the different situations and demonstrate a wide range of skills.

Reliable

Finally, are the results of the assessment reliable and consistent? A reliable assessment is one where if the same person took the test a number of times they would get much the same outcome.

The **VACSR** acronym is used widely by teaching and training professionals and acts as a guide to check the robustness of assessment methods.

[Practicality]

Addressing the five principles detailed above may mean the assessment process becomes overbearing, impractical and overburdened. Machin et al (2020) have added a sixth principle that considers this and asks the assessor to consider the practicality of the assessment.

Activity

Revisiting the methods of assessment listed previously, take three of the methods and evaluate VACRS for each method.

Method	Valid	Authentic	Current	Sufficient	Reliable

1.4 Explain how different assessment methods can be adapted to meet individual learner needs

The principles of assessment form a foundation on which we build the correct assessment method, to form accurate judgements on whether an individual has the right knowledge and understanding of a subject or skill. However, like most things, 'one size' does not fit all, so quite often methods need to be adjusted to support the needs of the learners.

Transparency of assessment methods is important for both the teacher and the learner. It is important that the learner understands what is expected of them and what they need to do to achieve, so that they can work towards that goal, seek the right support and ultimately complete the assessment.

Transparency is also key for the teacher so that the learners can join the journey, understand how the content of the taught sessions, the in-class work and the teaching strategies will all contribute to the overall assessment.

Sometimes this transparency has a different impact, depending on the nature and culture of certain learners. For example, some students will ask the question: 'will this count towards me passing the course?'. If the response is 'yes', then they will complete what is required. If the answer is 'no' then they may question the relevance.

Quite often we are presented with learners that need different levels of support and adjustments need to be made to the assessment methods to ensure everyone is given an equal opportunity.

Why would a learner's needs influence the assessment method?

Usually at application stage each new learner will declare if they have any learning needs that should be considered. This can include, but is not exclusive to, dyslexia, ADHD, a physical disability, or any medical conditions that may hinder learning.

Sometimes, the individual has been formally assessed by independent organisations who provide reports on the learning need and guidance on how they can be supported. This report provides key information on how to adapt the assessment methods to support the learner. For example, for dyslexic learners, it may mean more time in an exam or a slightly later submission date for an assignment. For other learners it may include a reader when completing an exam and a scribe to record the responses to answers. If they have not been formally assessed then you need to consider what support can be given that neither disadvantages the learner nor gives them an unfair advantage.

There are other instances where a learner may not be aware that they have a learning need when they begin the course and the teacher or trainer identifies certain traits that would indicate a need. This is not uncommon.

> **Case Study**
>
> The group you have been teaching for three months have submitted their first written assignment. It is 2,500 words and is based on the topic they have been studying since they started. In class there have been sessions on study skills and you have completed 1:1 tutorials with each individual to discuss the assignment and provide guidance. There has also been an opportunity to submit a draft assignment.
>
> One student, a mature student who has been out of education for 15 years, did not submit a draft assignment although did meet for the tutorials and was present for the study skills sessions. No learning needs have been disclosed but the learner did state that they disliked school and found it hard to complete the exams. They had avoided education since, however their job role now meant that they needed the qualification to continue in the role.
>
> You mark the assignment submitted and find that it does not meet the criteria by a significant margin. The structure of the assignment is fragmented, the writing is not clear with regular spelling mistakes and grammatical errors. The content of the assignment is disorganised and whilst there has been an attempt to try to answer the questions, the assignment misses key points. The lack of structure to the assignment is very concerning.
>
> - Consider how you would feedback on the assignment.
> - What support would you offer the learner when completing a resubmission?
> - Would you suggest any other support or interventions?
> - Does the assignment indicate there is a learning need and if so, what would you recommend next?

In the case study above there are indications that there may be a learning need and that extra support and possibly a formal diagnosis is required. An initial assessment for dyslexia would be a good starting point.

Adaptations to assessments that can be made if the learner has a formal diagnosis for a learning need include:

- extra time in exams
- later submission date
- a reader
- a scribe
- professional discussions to reduce assignment writing
- assistive technology.

Assessment methods for formal qualifications are more difficult to differentiate mainly because awarding bodies require the assessment to be consistent and fair to all. However, awarding bodies do have policies and guidance in place to support learners with specific needs and ensure academic integrity for all learners at all times.

To summarise this section, for adaptations to be made formally for learners with learning needs, a formal diagnosis is usually required. The method of assessment will determine the type of adaptations that can be implemented.

LO2 Understand how to involve learners and others in the assessment process

> 2.1 Explain why it is important to involve learners and others in the assessment process.
>
> 2.2 Explain the role and use of peer- and self-assessment in the assessment process.
>
> 2.3 Identify sources of information that should be made available to learners and others involved in the assessment process.

It is important that the learners are involved and supported through the assessment process. This section aims to explore how this involvement starts at the very beginning of their learning journey and what interventions the teacher or trainer can take to support this process.

2.1 Explain why it is important to involve learners and others in the assessment process

When starting a qualification very often the learner will ask whether there are exams. The methods of assessment may indicate to the new learner what level of commitment they have to put in and if the assessment method will suit their learning styles. Formal qualifications will indicate the assessment methods and how the criteria will be assessed. So, from the start the learner should have a clear indication of the assessment expectations.

It is very good practice to have an assessment plan before the start of any course or qualification. This plan will state the:

- assessment methods that are being used
- how they map to learning outcomes and criteria
- the dates of submission
- a plan of when the assessments will be launched within the programme.

Carefully consider how much detail to provide, as there is a fine balance between providing guidance and overwhelming learners at the start of the programme. Learners will often see assessments as a 'whole' rather than as the 'chunks' they complete as they progress through the programme.

Starting any course is often an anxious time for new students. If we revisit Maslow's Hierarchy of Needs (page 30) the lower levels are around physiological needs, followed by safety and then love and belonging. For a new student this means they will want to feel safe in the learning environment and want to belong. They will be concerned about making mistakes and sounding stupid. Our role as educators is to facilitate an environment where these risks are limited. A clear indication of assessment requirements does make that easier for the learner as they then know what they are signing up for.

To reinforce this need for clear information around assessment, complete the following activity.

Activity

1. Draw the Titanic, side profile and afloat.
2. Now mark your drawing using the following scores:

   a. 1 point for each funnel (max 4)
   b. 1 point for each porthole
   c. 5 points for including clouds
   d. 10 points for including both masts
   e. 6 points if you have added waves

Completing this activity without the scores (mark scheme) means you may have missed out on valuable points. If you had the mark scheme beforehand, it would have helped you achieve a higher score. Clarity of expectations in assessment is key; learners need to understand what is required of them, how they should present their assessment and the detail they need.

If the grading is more than a pass or fail, then more time is required to explain the grading system. For example:

- what is the difference between a pass and a merit or a merit and a distinction?
- how can you achieve the different percentage grade levels?

Preparing for summative assessment

Helping learners to prepare for assessments involves a range of teaching strategies that will support both their learning and their preparation. Some methods that you can use to support preparation for summative assessment include:

- Mock exams
- Draft assignments
- 1:1 tutorials
- Revision sessions
- Group tutorials
- Peer teaching
- Peer presentations
- Mini presentations

The more practice and preparation they have, the better placed they will be to succeed.

Learners also need to understand the consequences of not meeting assessment criteria, how they are able to respond to this, and the impact it will have on their studies. For example, in some non-examined assessments not meeting all of the 'Pass' criteria might prevent the learner from passing the course. But other assessment models may provide more flexibility. There may also be opportunities to resubmit non-examined assessment, or re-sit exams.

Awarding bodies and colleges also have processes for non-submission (not submitting an assessment on time) and for failing an assessment. Together with the launch of assessments, the deadline dates should be made clear, with proposed study plans to support the submission of the assessments.

Key Tips for launching assessments:

- Be clear about the submission date(s). Set the dates in advance of the course starting and point out if there are other key dates that may hinder, support or have an influence on the possible submission. (For example, holiday times, other assessment due dates or even aligning the date to the individual learner's events.) Do not change this date unless there are exceptional circumstances.

- Verbalise the assessment, read through it with the learners and rephrase or explain areas if the learners need more clarity.

- Discuss the assessment criteria. It is good practice to give the learners time in the session to read through the criteria, discuss it with peers and then ask questions and seek clarity.

- Check on the learners' understanding of what is required. It is also good practice to encourage learners to make notes next to the assessment criteria, linking what they have learned in class to the criteria.

- Be prepared to revisit this conversation with the students regularly as the deadline approaches.

- Where possible, include study time or assignment writing time into the schedule so that learners can start to complete non-examined assessments in the classroom with your support.

- Provide an outline of a plan to help learners contextualise their learning and link it to the criteria.

- Remind students of the actions required for them to take should they not be able to submit on time. This may include applying for an extension to their deadline. Awarding bodies have processes to support this.

- Learners will usually ask 'what if I fail?' Address this honestly and ensure they know how they can resubmit, what the terms of the resubmission are and if they have grades capped as a result of failing. Be transparent and honest at all times.

- Be clear about when a grade and feedback will be given to the learner. Consider the best feedback methods for each learner.

2.2 Explain the role and use of peer- and self-assessment in the assessment process

As much as a group will learn from you and your teaching strategies, they will also learn from one another. It is useful to harness this additional learning for assessment. However, you need to monitor it closely in case the learners have not gained the right information!

Peer-assessment is when one learner assesses another learner or small group of learners. They mutually support one another, build on what they have learned individually and collaboratively develop their own knowledge and skills.

Self-assessment is when an individual assesses their own work and checks what they have completed against the required criteria. It offers them time out to take stock, to review and to add or remove where necessary.

Each method offers the learner a different viewpoint from which to build their knowledge and skills. The pitfalls of both methods are around missing key criteria – 'you don't know what you don't know', so as a teacher, it is important you set the scene and provide accurate and supportive materials for learners to assess against. You will also need to check on the outcomes of the tasks you set that involve either of the methods.

Both are very good methods that can be used inside or outside of the classroom. However they should be used alongside other strategies to formatively check on learning and not used in isolation. To do so would be risky, as you would not have reassurance that learners had self- or peer-assessed against the right criteria with the right outcomes.

2.3 Identify sources of information that should be made available to learners and others involved in the assessment process

Some sources of information should be made available to learners to support and develop their understanding of what is required. Most awarding bodies will provide course specifications, learning outcomes and assessment criteria, including how they are broken down into achievable elements of the course. As a teacher, your role is to translate these requirements into a format that learners will be able to work towards and understand.

Sources of information that will support this process are:

- Course handbooks.
- Assignment handbooks.
- Access to any materials that learners might need to complete the assessment, such as case studies or scenarios.
- Digital learning platforms, ensuring they are up to date and contain information that supports completion of the assessment. (Examples of these platforms include Google Classroom, Moodle, or any other learning management system.)

- Study materials and links to information that support requirements such as textbooks, reference material and broader reading.

You should make sure that communication systems that your institution has in place are set up, should learners need advice outside of the classroom.

You should also set up a time when learners can access teacher support to discuss assessment.

Others involved in assessment

In addition to the learner, you will need to communicate the assessment process to any others within the organisation who are involved in assessment. This can include:

- other teachers marking the assessment
- people involved with administering assessment e.g. exams staff
- quality assurance personnel within the organisation, such as internal verifiers.

Internal verification is the process where someone within your organisation will check that the marking has been consistent and of the standard required throughout. An individual or a team may be assigned to this task depending on the organisation and/or the awarding body requirements. On occasion, the grade is not verified until it has been through this process. Learners need to be aware of this so that when they receive the outcomes of the assessment, they understand that it is not a FINAL grade until it has been internally verified. In some cases it may be an external verification that endorses the grade.

External verification occurs when the internal verification process has been completed. External verification is undertaken by the awarding body or validating organisation. As per the internal verification process, the external process will check on the quality and standard of the marking process and will endorse the grades that have been given. The main difference is simply that the external verifier is completely independent of the training provider or college. Quite often there will be recommendations on how to develop the marking process and how to improve it for the next cycle of assessments.

Both verification processes are key quality indicators that are in place to ensure the integrity, standard, and value of the qualification are maintained.

> ### Reflection
> - As a current teaching/training practitioner, do you involve your learners throughout the assessment process?
> - Do you have an assessment plan?
> - Do you have strategies for checking on the learners' understanding of what is required?
> - Do you effectively ask your learners to 'draw the titanic' – or do you give them the task and the scoring system?
> - How can you improve and build on your support of learners in their assessment journey?

LO3 Understand the role and use of constructive feedback in the assessment process

3.1 Describe key features of constructive feedback.

3.2 Explain how constructive feedback contributes to the assessment process.

3.3 Explain ways to give constructive feedback to learners.

To enable growth and development, constructive feedback is critical. It helps learners to realise their potential and move forward with their knowledge and understanding. People tend to thrive as they improve at something and become more effective.

Constructive feedback can be given formally or informally:

- formally, through assessment feedback
- informally within the classroom setting, or during a one-to-one
- it can be planned or more spontaneous.

This section aims to explore the power of constructive feedback and how it can shape and influence a learner.

3.1 Describe key features of constructive feedback

Constructive feedback supports a learner by focusing on what they need to do to develop. It is delivered to the individual in a non-judgemental, positive way. Constructive feedback enables a learner to move forward and build upon their current position.

'Feed forward' is a more current way to describe constructive feedback as it indicates movement and direction, suggesting that the feedback should be acted upon. This makes the learner more likely to improve or develop their skills moving forward.

A critical aspect of constructive feedback is the desire to support and guide the learner to progress their skills and knowledge, and build on what they have already achieved so far.

Reflection
Consider a time when you completed a task or an activity and wanted to know what others thought.

- Who did you ask and why?
- What information did you want to hear?
- What did you not want to hear?
- How open are you to constructive feedback?

How people respond to feedback can shape how the message should be delivered:

- Some people can be defensive, aim to challenge the feedback and explain why the situation is what it is.
- Other people can be quite open to feedback, prompting a more open and honest discussion that can lead to better learning outcomes in the future.

As a teacher or trainer, knowing how individuals respond to feedback is important. Knowing your learners can help you prepare and deliver the important messages effectively.

3.2 Explain how constructive feedback contributes to the assessment process

Constructive feedback contributes to assessment by providing the learner with information, support and guidance that will grow and develop their skills and knowledge.

For example, if a learner has not met the assessment criteria that has been set out, which of the following options would you choose?

1. Advise that the criteria had not been met.
2. Advise that the criteria had not been met and which aspects had been missed.
3. Advise that the criteria had not been met, highlight the areas that had been missed and ask questions to help fill those gaps.
4. Advise that the criteria had not been met, highlight the areas that had been missed and ask questions to help fill those gaps; and also point learners to where they can find more support and guidance to research and build on their knowledge and skills.

Clearly, Option 4 would provide the greatest amount of guidance for the learner. Of course, even comprehensive feedback like this requires that the learner is open to feedback and will consider and ultimately address what is being suggested.

Option 1 would be the absolute minimum and would not be deemed good practice.

Options 2, 3 and 4 provide learners with more detailed, constructive feedback. They offer the learner an opportunity to delve more deeply, explore what they have learned and how they can build on this learning. However, all three options require more time and effort on the teacher's and learner's behalf. So as teachers, we need to consider:

- how we can prepare learners to embrace constructive feedback and benefit from it
- how learners can interpret and act on the feedback
- how learners can translate this into their current learning journey and ultimately shape their learning.

This takes time and planning. The initial steps start right at the beginning of the course or qualification, when we set out our expectations of the learner. This is reinforced at the launch of the assessment activity, where we need to:

- Introduce the assignment/task that will be assessed.
- Remind learners to revisit the feedback from their previous assessed activity.
- Create time for learners to revisit the feedback.
- Discuss the new assessed activity and make links to previous feedback ('lessons learned').

3.3 Explain ways to give constructive feedback to learners

There are some good practice models to support providing constructive feedback. As stated previously, a teacher or trainer will need to create a learning environment that supports development, independent learning, and a desire to improve and build on skills and knowledge.

We covered the 'feedback sandwich' on page 96, when something negative is sandwiched between a couple of positives:

> *'When marking your assignment, I could see that you had read around the subject and understood what was required; it needed to be a bit more structured and fluent, but you managed to summarise the key points well.'*

Do you see how something that needs development has been sandwiched by two positive comments? This keeps the feedback constructive. However, it risks the development point being lost in the discussion, so the learner may choose to focus on the positives as opposed to the developmental aspect. Alternatively, it could go in the opposite direction and the learner focuses solely on the developmental point and loses the positives.

Activity

Look at the following and what do you see?

1 + 1 = 2

1 + 2 = 3

1 + 3 = 5

1 + 4 = 5

My guess is that your eye was drawn to the incorrect sum in the middle. How would you mark the example above if you were teaching maths? How would you give feedback to that learner? Something like this?:

1 + 1 = 2 ✓

1 + 2 = 3 ✓

1 + 3 = 5 x

1 + 4 = 5 ✓

Isn't it incredible how we are drawn to the incorrect sum. This gives us an insight into how learners process feedback. The fact is that 75% of the above was correct. However, we do tend to focus on the 25%.

In some contexts it may be right to focus on what is incorrect. However, as teachers and trainers we need to ensure there is balance. If we go too far one way we risk learners becoming too self-critical, and failing to recognise the good things they are doing that supports their development.

A teacher's role is to ensure there is a balance between striving to move forward but also building on what is already established. So, constructive feedback is not always about highlighting the aspects that are not correct, but building on the areas that are meeting the criteria but that can be moved further forward. This is where we support the realising of potential and help the learner create, develop and master skills, knowledge and understanding. This can help them to develop beyond their expectations. This is an example of 'feed-forward'.

So, how do we give feedback? Listed below are the most common methods.

Feedback method	Advantages	Disadvantages	Possible solutions
Verbal (via tutorial or one-to-one meeting)	Allows the learner to seek clarification and ask questions. Gives the teacher the opportunity to explain in more detail.	Not recorded. Time-consuming for larger groups.	Record it or encourage the learner to make notes. Peer discussions.
Written (on assignment or a front sheet)	Permanent record for the learner. Can be revisited by the learner after the feedback is given.	No opportunity to clarify what is being suggested. May misunderstand the feedback that is being given.	Follow up with a tutorial to discuss the feedback.
Informal Feedback (in the classroom)	This can be instant, such as a thumbs up, or a word of support and affirmation, and provides an opportunity to praise and reward on the spot.	May not be recognised by the individual. May not be specific enough to enable a change of behaviour or attitude.	Make a note and repeat the feedback where possible.

Further Tips to giving Effective Feedback

Timing

Ensure the learner is ready for feedback and that they can process it. This may mean preparing learners in advance of the feedback and giving them strategies to deal with it, e.g. how to act upon it and how to explore it further.

Give them time to ask and clarify what is meant, and maybe even an opportunity to challenge it. They may think that they are already where they need to be, so constructive feedback may not be expected. Tutorials after written feedback is good practice, so that the learner can discuss the content of the feedback and move forward with it through action-plans.

Relevance

Be specific with feedback and make it relevant to their ability and what is within their control. There may be several aspects that the learner needs to develop but be selective rather than overwhelm.

What's in it for me? (WIIFM)

Demonstrate the benefits to the learner of acting upon the feedback given. For example:

> *'if the learner becomes more consistent with their referencing, and uses more underpinning knowledge to support ideas and opinions, they will move up a grade, or achieve a distinction'.*

Spell out how the improvements will provide the learner with clear benefits and how it will help them move forward.

LO4 Understand requirements for keeping records of assessment in education and training

> 4.1 Explain the need to keep records of assessment of learning.
>
> 4.2 Summarise the requirements for keeping records of assessment in an organisation.

Record keeping is essential for tracking a learner's progress against outcomes and ultimately recognising the completion of a qualification. Record keeping is critical throughout the duration of a qualification – it starts as soon as the learner applies to attend and lasts for up to five years after they have left.

4.1 Explain the need to keep records of assessment of learning

4.2 Summarise the requirements for keeping records of assessment in an organisation

There are a variety of parties who are interested in assessment of learning records. They include:

- the learner
- the teacher/trainer
- the teaching team
- the internal verifier
- the external verifier
- the college or training provider quality team
- the awarding body.

Each party will have a different interest in different records, and a different reason for keeping them.

	Reason for keeping records	Type of record
The learner	Tracking their progress and understanding what is required to pass and achieve the qualification. Completion of assessments to gain certification.	Application form Individual learning plans (ILPs) Criteria tracking form Authentication statements Completed assessments
The teacher	As above. Ensuring the learner is on target to achieve the qualification and identifying at an early stage if there are any issues with the progress of the learner.	Attendance and punctuality Criteria tracking form Feedback and marking sheets
The teaching team	Very often, a learner is taught by several teachers, and it is critical that records are maintained so that all teachers can support and track the progress of groups and individuals. Records of assessment need to be retained for 3-5 years depending on the awarding body requirements.	Completed and marked assessments Criteria tracking form Feedback and marking sheets Course evaluation
The internal verifier	To show that the verification process was completed in a timely manner, and work was thoroughly checked for consistency and standardisation of marking.	Completed and marked assessments Criteria tracking form Internal verification record
The institution's quality team	To demonstrate that quality was maintained, and any developmental actions identified previously by the external verifier have been acted upon. Funding requirements.	Completed and marked assessments Criteria tracking form Internal verification record External verifier's report from previous group
The external verifier	Receives the tracking record that shows completed assessments, records of internal verification and can then select which areas to externally verify. Records show that the EV process was thorough, fair and in line with awarding body requirements.	Completed and marked assessments Criteria tracking form Internal verification record/report Course evaluation
The awarding body	Once the verification process has been completed the certification process can be instigated. The awarding body needs all records to be in place to be reassured that all quality aspects have been completed.	Completed and marked assessments Criteria tracking form Internal verification record Claim for certification IV Report EV Report

GDPR legislation means there are also legal requirements on how records are kept, where the information is stored and the timeframe for keeping the records. Be aware of these requirements and check with the awarding bodies, as some of their requirements may differ. Do make sure that records are stored confidentially and securely.

When appropriate, records should be disposed in a confidential way, such as shredding or using confidential waste companies.

Evaluation of teaching and learning

Assessment and evaluation are different and yet often confused.

- Assessment is the checking of learning.
- Evaluation is the checking of the process.

Let's reflect on that. You will have experienced the process of evaluation on many occasions. For example, at the end of a course you will have been asked about your thoughts of the course. You may have been asked questions such as:

- Was it easy to sign up for the course?
- Was the training good?
- Did the course meet your objectives?
- Was it what you expected?

This type of evaluation checks that the methods and strategies used to support the learning process have met the needs of the learners.

Evaluation forms can help identify any areas for improvement, inform the planning of the next course, provide valuable feedback to the tutor and be used to promote the course to future audiences.

Recording evaluations is important and supports the quality and integrity of the programme. Awarding bodies will ask for this information and it also offers learners the opportunity to contribute to the development of the programme or course.

References

Chapter 1

Coffield, F, Moseley, D, Hall, E, & Ecclestone, K 2004, Should we be using learning styles in post-16 education?; what research has to say to practice. Learning and Skills Research Centre.

Coffield, F. (2013) Learning Styles: time to move on, opinion piece. National College for School Leadership.

Hill, C. and Howard, K., 2020. Symbiosis: The curriculum and the classroom. John Catt.

The power of yet | Carol S Dweck | TEDxNorrköping https://www.youtube.com/watch?v=J-swZaKN2Ic	tinyurl.com/3yan8t32	
Anindya Kundu: The boost students need to overcome obstacles | TEDTalk https://www.youtube.com/watch?v=h9deGh8_tEc	tinyurl.com/52ymudzr	
The Power of Teaching | Matt Burton Exclusive | The National College https://nationalcollege.com/webinars/power-of-teaching	tinyurl.com/rtj63tbp	
Rita Pierson: Every kid needs a champion | TED Talk https://www.youtube.com/watch?v=SFnMTHhKdkw	tinyurl.com/tm9afpcc	

Howard, K. & Hill, C. (2021). Curriculum sequencing – How to decide what to teach and when. Available from Curriculum sequencing – How to decide what to teach and when (teachwire.net)

A Beginner's Guide To Lesson Planning - Engage Education (engage-education.com)

https://www.gov.uk/government/publications/prevent-duty-guidance/prevent-duty-guidance-for-further-education-institutions-in-england-and-wales

www.set.et-foundation.co.uk

http://www.et-foundation/

www.cla.co.uk

www.channel4.com/programmes/the-school-that-tried-to-end-racism

https://www.ted.com/

http://www.adhdaware.org.uk/

http://www.nhs.uk/conditions/autism/what-is-autism

http://www.autism.org.uk/

http://www.dyscalculiaassociation.uk/

http://www.bdadyslexia.org.uk/

http://www.mint-hr.com/mumford/

http://www.teachertoolkit.co.uk/

Maslow's Hierarchy (Various pages), Honey & Mumford (P33) from BATES. B. (2019) Learning Theories Simplified, Second Edition. Sage Publishing. London.

Chapter 2

Dale, E. (1969). Audiovisual methods in teaching (3rd ed.). New York: Dryden Press

Lightbody, B. (2009) Outstanding teaching and learning 14-19. Collegenet Publications. West Yorkshire.

Deci, E.L. and Ryan, R.M., (2008). Self-determination theory: A macrotheory of human motivation, development, and health. Canadian psychology/Psychologie canadienne, 49(3), p.182.

Bloom, B.S., (1956). Taxonomy of. Educational Objectives: Handbook I: Cognitive domain. New York: David McKay

Anderson, L.W. & Krathwohl, D.R. (Eds.) (2001). A taxonomy for Learning, teaching, and assessing: Arevision of Bloom's taxonomy of educational objectives. New York: Addison Wesley Longman

Rolfe., G., Freshwater, D., and Jasper, M. (2001) Critical reflection in nursing and the helping professions: a user's guide. Basingstoke, Palgrave Macmillan

Brookfield, S.D. (2001) Developing critical thinkers: Challenging adults to explore alternative ways of thinking and acting. San Francisco, CA: Jossey-Bass.

Chapter 3

Machin, L. Hindmarch, D. Murray, S. Richardson, T. (2020) A complete guide to the Level 4 Certificate in Education and Training, Third Edition, Critical Publishing. St Albans

Black, P. & Wiliam, D. (2014) Inside the Black Box: Raising Standards Through Classroom Assessment. King's College London.

Wiliam, D. (2018) https://tinyurl.com/mpebjh9y

Appendix 1
Artificial Intelligence (AI)

Artificial Intelligence, usually abbreviated to **AI**, is defined by the Oxford Languages Dictionary as *the theory and development of computer systems able to perform tasks normally requiring human intelligence.* For most people, whether we like it or not, AI is already embedded in many day-to-day tasks, very often without us even realising it.

- If you have a smartphone, predictive text is used to spell words correctly, or predict which words could be next in your sentence.
- Smartphone cameras use AI to process images to provide better results.
- Search engines and recommendation engines (e.g. Netflix, Spotify) all use AI to give results that are likely to appeal to you personally.
- In cars, route-planning GPS software use AI to predict the best route in real-time.
- Email spam filters, and fraud detection in banking apps, all use AI.

Much of this technology has been around for some time and did not cause too much concern. However, in 2023 OpenAI made ChatGPT 3 available to the general public, and brought AI more clearly into the public's consciousness. This is because ChatGPT, and other similar software from other companies, is generative AI. ChatGPT and others are able to analyse documents,, answer questions and write extremely well. There has been rapid progress in generative AI which has led to questions about the future and the impact it will have on all sorts of human activities.

For education, we need to consider how AI can support learning as well as how it might hinder it. Assistive technology, and any programmes that support learning needs and provide enhancement to disadvantaged learners, is definitely a step in the right direction. However, learners are potentially able to ask AI to write assignments on their behalf. This is a hazard, as it can often be hard or even impossible for a teacher or trainer to decipher the work of the individual.

The benefits

As a teacher, my organisation has subscribed to TeacherMatic, which is AI technology that has proved to be a timesaver when planning a taught session. To support this section of the book, it seemed logical to demonstrate the use of AI, so in preparing this section we asked generative AI software: What are the benefits of using AI as a teacher? This was the response:

As a teacher, developing critical thinking skills about AI can greatly benefit your understanding and implementation of this technology in the classroom. To start, it is important to stay informed about the latest AI advancements and their potential impact on education. Familiarize yourself with the different subfields of AI, such as machine learning and natural language processing, to gain a deeper understanding of how these technologies work.

Some points to look at when reading the AI-generated paragraph above:

- American spelling
- A logical response
- Reads well
- Useful points made to move learning forward

All are great benefits, but this paragraph is only a starting point. Using this to support a taught session would be useful but it would not be standalone material. You would need to back up these points with key knowledge:

- What is 'machine learning' and how does it work?
- What is 'natural language processing' and how does it work?

Of course, we can ask the AI these questions, which can often save time compared to conducting research using a search engine. However, whilst AI can be a time saver, we still need to organise information and put in further work to gain a deeper understanding of a subject or topic.

The pitfalls of AI

Flip the advantages above and think how they may also hinder the learning process. One key issue is that an AI's response is always stated as fact – but in fact they can often get things wrong. So relying on factual information supplied by AI is very risky.

Spotting when a learner has used AI can be tricky, but knowing the learner's normal writing style you can look for hints that there may have used AI – for example, the American spelling above or the use of words that would not be normally used by the learner. You can also use generative AI to spot its own work. For example, Chat-GPT is quite good at guessing whether it is the likely source of an essay. However this would not necessarily work if you used a different generative AI tool.

Taking time to explain to learners how to use AI effectively, and in ways that can enhance learning, is far more proactive than simply ignoring the potential use of AI. We all have exposure to AI, whether we like it or not, and some learners will be far more attuned to its use to support their development. Therefore, it is important to invest time in becoming familiar with its use.

Moving forward with AI

Be sure to have a discussion about AI with your learners. Spend time becoming familiar with AI yourself, how it is used within your organisation and what advice there is from your awarding body or other organisations you work with.

Perhaps set an activity for learners to research the AI that is available to them and present it back to their peers. Demonstrate the AI tools that you use and show how it benefits your planning and preparation and how they can use it as a starting point for their own learning. Take time to become familiar with AI and make it part of your development.

Sustainability

Education and training can play a vital role in tackling climate change by including sustainability within its curricula. As we are often teaching future generations, it is only right that we consider the changes we can make to sustain a better environment for all. Most areas of industry and business will have considered their approaches to sustainability over recent years. With concerns about the effects of climate change growing, all new qualification specifications will have sustainability as a core element for learners to understand within their subject.

It is important for a new teacher or trainer to consider sustainability in their own practice, such as not overusing the photocopier, creating resources that are reuseable and cutting down on waste. Alongside this, it is also important to understand how sustainability relates to your subject specialism and what the latest technologies or developments are within your field.

For example, as a teacher of travel and tourism, I am very aware of the environmental impacts of tourism, whether that be carbon dioxide and other emissions from airplanes and cruise ships, or the sustainable approaches that hotels and visitor attractions can choose to invest in for energy efficiency. There are other sustainability challenges and solutions within other sectors. Your challenge is to seek out information and examples from within your area of specialism and identify what would be appropriate and practical to include when teaching.

Support for teachers is available:

- The Education Training Foundation (ETF), host numerous online webinars and trainings specifically on teaching about sustainability.
- In December 2023, the government produced a document on 'Sustainability and climate change strategy: our progression so far (December 2023), which is a useful starting point and highlights some case studies that may suit your educational requirements.

www.et-foundation.co.uk/resources/esd/esd-resources/esd-in-different-subject-areas/

www.gov.uk/government/publications/sustainability-and-climate-change-strategy

Appendix 2

By using Bloom's Taxonomy's principles, and the appropriate set of verbs (see below), you can develop activities to support growth. For example, think about how the following different objectives could support development:

- List five main organs of the body.
- Explain what the five main organs of the body do.
- Differentiate between each of the five main organs.
- Evaluate the importance of these five organs.

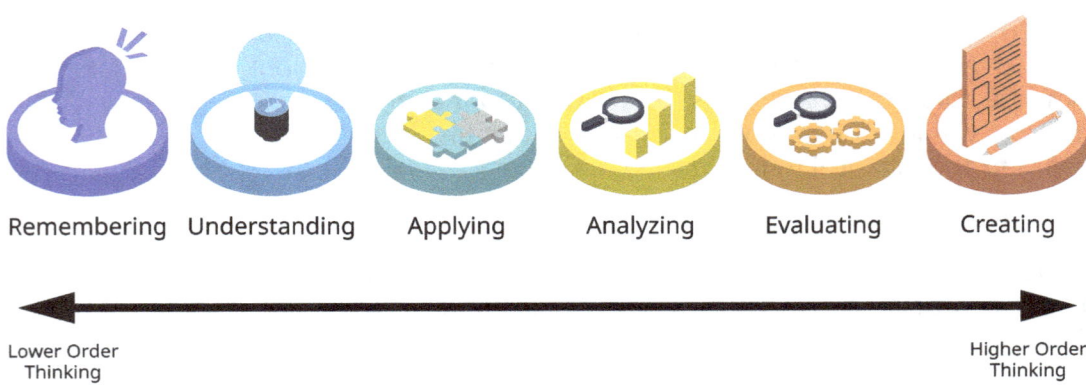

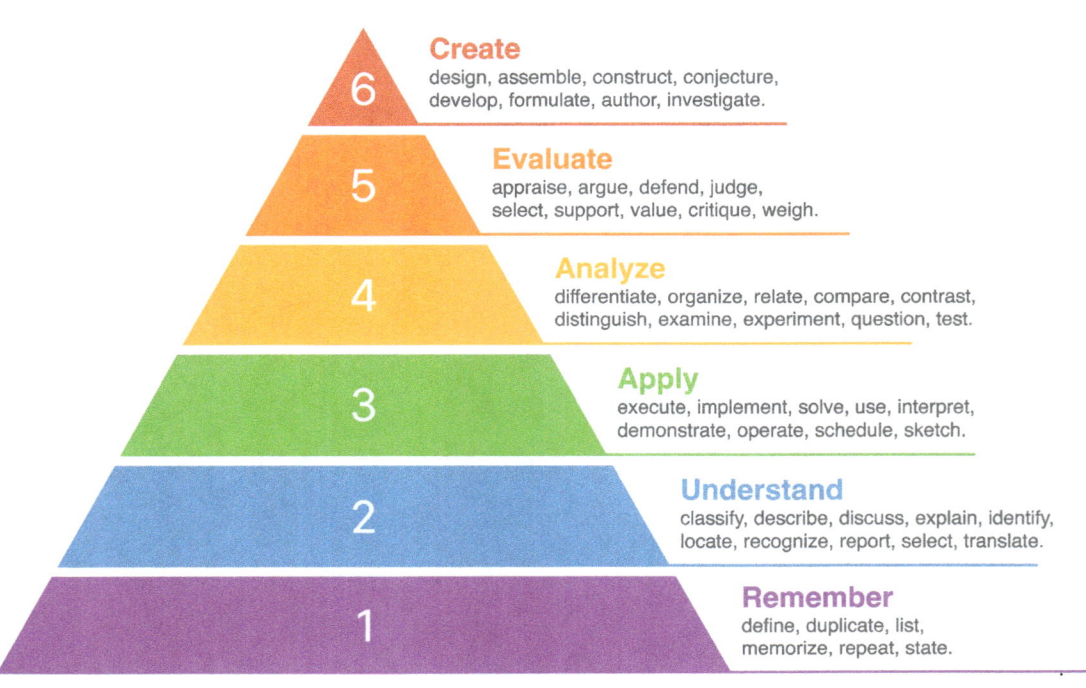

Index

A
accidents, 16
active learning, 60, 62–63, 65, 77, 88
activities
    energiser, 86
    final, 103
    fun, 81
    individual, 88
    leadership, 50
    maths-based, 37
    quick, 92
    scaffolded, 59, 70
    social, 51
    starter, 79
    team, 29
ADHD, 31–32, 37, 110
assessment
    internal, 53
    peer, 96
assessment criteria, 115, 118
Assessment for Learning (AfL), 105
assessment methods, 70–71, 76, 85, 88, 106–12
Assessment of Learning (AoL), 105, 122
assessment process, 112, 115–16
assessments, adaptations, 111
autism, 31–32
Autism Spectrum Disorder, 32
awarding bodies, 25, 52–54, 56, 106, 111, 114–16, 122–24

B
behaviour
    acceptable, 24
    anti-social, 68
    discriminatory, 68
    disruptive, 11, 68
    encouraging, 46
    managing, 46
behavioural issues, 57
Bloom's Taxonomy, 60, 72
body language, 93–94, 100
boundaries, 4, 6, 12–13, 42, 52, 55–56
    establishing, 3, 12
    personal, 12
    physical, 55
Bradley Lightbody's Diamond Lesson plan, 62
Bribery Act, 15, 20
Brookfield's Reflective Lenses, 98–99
bullying, 42, 50, 56

C
Children Act, 15, 17
Children and Social Work Act, 15, 17
children and vulnerable adults, 18, 39, 41
CLA (Copyright Licencing Agency), 20
classroom management, 10, 13, 44, 46–47, 49, 69, 100
codes of practice, 15, 22
Coffield, 33
cone of experience, 60
constructive feedback, 30, 90, 93, 95, 102, 117–21
COSHH (Control of Substances Hazardous to Health), 15–16
Counter-Terrorism and Security Act, 19
Covid pandemic, 61
cyberbullying, 42

D
Dale, 60–61
Dangerous Occurrences Regulations, 15–16
Data Protection Act, 15, 17
DBS (Disclosure and Barring Service), 18
Deci and Ryan, 71
Department for Education (DfE), 19, 25
Diagnostic assessment, 30, 104
Diamond Lesson Plan, 63
Disclosure and Barring Service (DBS), 18
discrimination, 18, 25–26, 28–29
diversity, 10, 19, 23, 25, 28–29, 68, 70
dyscalculia, 31–32, 37–38
dyslexia, 31–32, 36–38, 110–11
dyspraxia, 31–32, 38

E
Education Act, 15, 19
Education and Training Foundation (ETF), 25, 52
energisers, 81, 87
equality, 10, 19, 23, 25, 27–29
Equality Act, 15, 18, 25–26, 28
equality and diversity, 18, 23, 25, 28–29
evaluation, 54, 72, 86, 123–24
experiential learning, 88
external quality assurance, 53
external verification, 116

F
features of inclusive teaching, 4, 59
feedback, 63, 73–74, 91, 93, 95–101, 111, 114, 117–21, 124
    effective, 58
    external, 93
    giving, 97
    peer, 50
    positive, 101
feedback sandwich, 96, 119
feedforward, 96, 117
flipped learning, 44
formal diagnosis, 111
formative assessment, 70, 85, 104–5
Freedom of Information Act, 15, 20
furniture, 39, 41

G
GDPR, 15, 17, 124
ground rules, 42, 48, 50, 68, 74–75
group activities, 100
group juggle, 84
growth mindset, 30, 45

H
holistic assessment, 106
Honey & Mumford, 33

I
icebreakers, 80, 87
inclusive learning environment, 24–25, 58, 60, 75, 89
inclusive space, 27–28, 74
Independent Safeguarding Authority (ISA), 18

Individual learning plans (ILPs), 123
Information Commissioners Office, 17
information processing, 32
initial assessment, 76, 104, 111
interactive learning, 29
internal verification, 116, 123

K
keeping records, 102, 122–23

L
learners
    chatting, 47
    disruptive, 46
    dyslexic, 110
    neurodiverse, 37
learning activities, 43, 70, 81
learning activity ideas, 81
learning environment
    positive, 13
    productive, 50
    safe, 6
learning experience, 11, 33–35
learning plan, 4, 76–77
learning styles, 33–34, 36–37, 59, 112
legislation, 7, 10–11, 15, 17, 21–22, 24
lesson plan, 44, 60, 64, 77, 87–92, 98, 106
lesson plan formats, 86
lesson planning, 37, 43, 60, 62, 101
lesson plan proforma, 43, 78
literacy, 66
long term memories, 71, 87

M
Maslow's Hierarchy, 30, 38–39, 42, 49
methods of assessment, 103, 107
microteach, 58, 64, 71, 77, 79, 86–89, 91–92, 94–96, 98–101, 106
mobile phones, 13–14, 42
motivation, 31, 35–36, 71–74

N
neurodiversity, 2, 32
non-examined assessments, 114
numeracy, 19, 66

O
Ofsted, 25, 42, 74

P
passive learning, 60–61, 65, 81
pastoral support, 10, 48
peer-assessment, 96, 115
plenary activities, 84, 87
policies and procedures, 7, 10–11, 14, 21–22, 42, 49–50
PowerPoint, 37
prior knowledge, 26, 28, 33, 72, 76, 79, 82, 86, 89, 92, 100
procedures, 7, 10–11, 14, 21–22, 32, 42–43, 49–50, 53, 57
professionals in education and training, 52
protected characteristics, 25–29

Q
question types, 94

R
radicalisation, 19

records, 16, 20, 31, 65, 99, 102–3, 110, 120, 122–24
records of assessment, 122–23
RIDDOR, 15–16
roles and responsibilities, 7, 10, 13–15, 17–18, 21, 46, 55, 57

S
safeguarding, 10, 17, 19, 21, 39, 42, 52
Safeguarding & Vulnerable Groups Act, 15, 18
self-actualisation, 30, 49
self-assessment, 96, 115
sequencing, 44, 62
session
    creating, 72
    delivered, 94
    induction, 31
    missed, 81
    planned, 60
    previous, 80
    regular, 29
sexual orientation, 17–18, 27–28
skills
    analytical, 66
    core, 106
    employability, 50
    interpersonal, 73
    literacy, 32
    mathematical, 32
    numeracy, 66
    problem-solving, 66
    social, 66
    study, 111
SMART acronyms, 36, 73
Social Work Act, 15, 17
spaced retrieval, 87
starter activities, 79
starter activity, 79, 81, 84, 87
stereotyping, 25, 28
summative assessment, 71, 105, 113
supportive learning environment, 39, 43, 49
support plan, 38
swearing, 12, 75

T
teacher activities, 81
teachers, newly-qualified, 42
teacher training, 25
team-building activities, 83
tutorials, 73, 111, 114, 120–21

V
VAK questionnaire, 33
verification processes, 116, 123
vulnerable adults, 18, 39, 41

W
work-based training, 59

www.ingramcontent.com/pod-product-compliance
Lightning Source LLC
Chambersburg PA
CBHW081918090526
44590CB00019B/3392